BELOVED

Toni Morrison

SPARKNOTES

Contributors: Selena Ward, Pelagia Horgan, Katie Mannheimer, Sarah Friedberg

Note: This SparkNote uses the Penguin Great Books of the 20th Century edition of *Beloved*. While the edition falls into three numbered parts, each part contains many smaller sections, which are unnamed and unnumbered. For the sake of simplicity, this SparkNote refers to these smaller sections as chapters and has assigned each a number. The numbering system runs continuously throughout the book's three parts.

This edition published by Spark Publishing

Spark Publishing
A Division of SparkNotes LLC
76 9th Avenue, 11th Floor
New York, NY 10011

ISBN 1-58663-418-6

Text design by Rhea Braunstein
Text composition by Jackson Typesetting

Printed and bound in the United States of America

01 02 03 04 05 SN 9 8 7 6 5 4 3 2 1

RRD-C

http://www.sparknotes.com

INTRODUCTION

Stopping to Buy SparkNotes on a Snowy Evening

Whose words these are you *think* you know.
Your paper's due tomorrow, though;
We're glad to see you stopping here
To get some help before you go.

Lost your course? You'll find it here.
Face tests and essays without fear.
Between the words, good grades at stake:
Get great results throughout the year.

Once school bells caused your heart to quake
As teachers circled each mistake.
Use SparkNotes and no longer weep,
Ace every single test you take.

Yes, books are lovely, dark, and deep,
But only what you grasp you keep,
With hours to go before you sleep,
With hours to go before you sleep.

CONTENTS

CONTEXT

Toni Morrison was born Chloe Anthony Wofford in 1931 and spent the first years of her life in Ohio. She received an undergraduate degree in English from Howard University and completed a master's program at Cornell. When many of her classmates had difficulty pronouncing her uncommon first name, she changed it to Toni (a derivative of her middle name). In 1958, she married Harold Morrison, an architect from Jamaica, and the couple had two sons. They divorced six years later. After pursuing an academic career teaching English at Howard, Morrison became an editor at Random House, where she specialized in black fiction. At the same time, she began building a body of creative work that, in 1993, would make her the first African-American woman to receive the Nobel Prize for Literature. Her 1970 novel *The Bluest Eye* was followed by *Sula* in 1974, which secured Morrison a nomination for the National Book Award. In 1977, Morrison won the National Book Critics Circle Award for her book *Song of Solomon.* Her other works include *Tar Baby* (1981), *Jazz* (1992), *Paradise* (1998), and, of course, *Beloved.* That novel, considered by many to be her best, won the Pulitzer Prize in 1988. Today, Morrison is the Robert F. Goheen Professor in the Council of Humanities at Princeton University, where she conducts undergraduate workshops in creative writing.

Set during the Reconstruction era in 1873, *Beloved* centers on the powers of memory and history. For the former slaves in the novel, the past is a burden that they desperately and willfully try to forget. Yet for Sethe, the protagonist of the novel, memories of slavery are inescapable. They continue to haunt her, literally, in the spirit of her deceased daughter. Eighteen years earlier, Sethe had murdered this daughter in order to save her from a life of slavery. Morrison borrowed the event from the real story of Margaret Garner, who, like Sethe, escaped from slavery in Kentucky and murdered her child when slave catchers caught up with her in Ohio. *Beloved* straddles the line between fiction and history; from the experiences of a single family, Morrison creates a powerful commentary on the psychological and historical legacy of slavery.

Part of Morrison's project in *Beloved* is to recuperate a history that had been lost to the ravages of forced silences and willed forgetfulness. Morrison writes Sethe's story with the voices of a people who historically have been denied the power of language. *Beloved* also contains a didactic element. From Sethe's experience, we learn that before a stable future can be created, we must confront and understand the "ghosts" of the past. Morrison suggests that, like Sethe, contemporary American readers must confront the history of slavery in order to address its legacy, which manifests itself in ongoing racial discrimination and discord.

Morrison once said that she wanted to help create a canon of black work, noting that black writers too often have to pander to a white audience when they should be able to concentrate on the business of writing instead. Many readers believe Morrison's novels go a long way toward the establishment of her envisioned tradition. The poetic, elegant style of her writing in *Beloved* panders to no one. Morrison challenges and requires the reader to accept her on her own terms.

PLOT OVERVIEW

Beloved begins in 1873 in Cincinnati, Ohio, where Sethe, a former slave, has been living with her eighteen-year-old daughter Denver. Sethe's mother-in-law, Baby Suggs, lived with them until her death eight years earlier. Just before Baby Suggs's death, Sethe's two sons, Howard and Buglar, ran away. Sethe believes they fled because of the malevolent presence of an abusive ghost that has haunted their house at 124 Bluestone Road for years. Denver, however, likes the ghost, which everyone believes to be the spirit of her dead sister.

On the day the novel begins, Paul D, whom Sethe has not seen since they worked together on Mr. Garner's Sweet Home plantation in Kentucky approximately twenty years earlier, stops by Sethe's house. His presence resurrects memories that have lain buried in Sethe's mind for almost two decades. From this point on, the story will unfold on two temporal planes. The present in Cincinnati constitutes one plane, while a series of events that took place around twenty years earlier, mostly in Kentucky, constitutes the other. This latter plane is accessed and described through the fragmented flashbacks of the major characters. Accordingly, we frequently read these flashbacks several times, sometimes from varying perspectives, with each successive narration of an event adding a little more information to the previous ones.

From these fragmented memories, the following story begins to emerge: Sethe, the protagonist, was born in the South to an African mother she never knew. When she is thirteen, she is sold to the Garners, who own Sweet Home and practice a comparatively benevolent kind of slavery. There, the other slaves, who are all men, lust after her but never touch her. Their names are Sixo, Paul D, Paul A, Paul F, and Halle. Sethe chooses to marry Halle, apparently in part because he has proven generous enough to buy his mother's freedom by hiring himself out on the weekends. Together, Sethe and Halle have two sons, Howard and Buglar, as well as a baby daughter whose name we never learn. When she leaves Sweet Home, Sethe is also pregnant with a fourth child. After the eventual death of the proprietor, Mr. Garner, the widowed Mrs. Garner asks her sadistic, vehemently racist brother-in-law to help her run the farm. He is known to the slaves as schoolteacher, and his oppressive presence makes life on the plantation even more unbearable than it had been before. The slaves decide to run.

Schoolteacher and his nephews anticipate the slaves' escape, however, and capture Paul D and Sixo. Schoolteacher kills Sixo and brings Paul D back to Sweet Home, where Paul D sees Sethe for what he believes will be the last time. She is still intent on running, having already sent her children ahead to her mother-in-law Baby Suggs's house in Cincinnati. Invigorated by the recent capture, schoolteacher's nephews seize Sethe in the barn and violate her, stealing the milk her body is storing for her infant daughter. Unbeknownst to Sethe, Halle is watching the event from a loft above her, where he lies frozen with horror. Afterward, Halle goes mad: Paul D sees him sitting by a churn with butter slathered all over his face. Paul D, meanwhile, is forced to suffer the indignity of wearing an iron bit in his mouth.

When schoolteacher finds out that Sethe has reported his and his nephews' misdeeds to Mrs. Garner, he has her whipped severely, despite the fact that she is pregnant. Swollen and scarred, Sethe nevertheless runs away, but along the way she collapses from exhaustion in a forest. A white girl, Amy Denver, finds her and nurses her back to health. When Amy later helps Sethe deliver her baby in a boat, Sethe names this second daughter Denver after the girl who helped her. Sethe receives further help from Stamp Paid, who rows her across the Ohio River to Baby Suggs's house. Baby Suggs cleans Sethe up before allowing her to see her three older children.

Sethe spends twenty-eight wonderful days in Cincinnati, where Baby Suggs serves as an unofficial preacher to the black community. On the last day, however, schoolteacher comes for Sethe to take her and her children back to Sweet Home. Rather than surrender her children to a life of dehumanizing slavery, she flees with them to the woodshed and tries to kill them. Only the third child, her older daughter, dies, her throat having been cut with a handsaw by Sethe. Sethe later arranges for the baby's headstone to be carved with the word "Beloved." The sheriff takes Sethe and Denver to jail, but a group of white abolitionists, led by the Bodwins, fights for her release. Sethe returns to the house at 124, where Baby Suggs has sunk into a deep depression. The community shuns the house, and the family continues to live in isolation.

Meanwhile, Paul D has endured torturous experiences in a chain gang in Georgia, where he was sent after trying to kill Brandywine, a slave owner to whom he was sold by schoolteacher. His traumatic experiences have caused him to lock away his memories, emotions, and ability to love in the "tin tobacco box" of his heart. One day, a fortuitous rainstorm allows Paul D and the other chain gang members to escape. He travels northward by following the spring flowers as they blossom. Years later, he ends up on Sethe's porch in Cincinnati.

Paul D's arrival at 124 commences the series of events taking place in the present time frame. Prior to moving in, Paul D chases the house's resident ghost away, which makes the already lonely Denver resent him from the start. Sethe and Paul D look forward to a promising future together, until one day, on their way home from a carnival, they encounter a strange young woman sleeping near the steps of 124. Most of the characters believe that the woman—who calls herself Beloved—is the embodied spirit of Sethe's dead daughter, and the novel provides a wealth of evidence supporting this interpretation. Denver develops an obsessive attachment to Beloved, and Beloved's attachment to Sethe is equally if not more intense. Paul D and Beloved hate each other, and Beloved controls Paul D by moving him around the house like a rag doll and by seducing him against his will.

When Paul D learns the story of Sethe's "rough choice"—her infanticide—he leaves 124 and begins sleeping in the basement of the local church. In his absence, Sethe and Beloved's relationship becomes more intense and exclusive. Beloved grows increasingly abusive, manipulative, and parasitic, and Sethe is obsessed with satisfying Beloved's demands and making her understand why she murdered her. Worried by the way her mother is wasting away, Denver leaves the premises of 124 for the first time in twelve years in order to seek help from Lady Jones, her former teacher. The community provides the family with food and eventually organizes under the leadership of Ella, a woman who had worked on the Underground Railroad and helped with Sethe's escape, in order to exorcise Beloved from 124. When they arrive at Sethe's house, they see Sethe on the porch with Beloved, who stands smiling at them, naked and pregnant. Mr. Bodwin, who has come to 124 to take Denver to her new job, arrives at the house. Mistaking him for schoolteacher, Sethe runs at Mr. Bodwin with an ice pick. She is restrained, but in the confusion Beloved disappears, never to return.

Afterward, Paul D comes back to Sethe, who has retreated to Baby Suggs's bed to die. Mourning Beloved, Sethe laments, "She was my best thing." But Paul D replies, "You your best thing, Sethe." The novel then ends with a warning that "[t]his is not a story to pass on." The town, and even the residents of 124, have forgotten Beloved "[l]ike an unpleasant dream during a troubling sleep."

CHARACTER LIST

Sethe—Sethe, the protagonist of *Beloved,* is a proud and independent woman who is extremely devoted to her children. Though she barely knew her own mother, Sethe's motherly instincts are her most striking characteristic. Unwilling to relinquish her children to the physical, emotional, sexual, and spiritual trauma she endured as a slave at Sweet Home, she attempts to murder them in an act of motherly love and protection. She remains haunted by this and other scarring events in her past, which she tries, in vain, to repress.

Denver—Sethe's youngest child, Denver is the most dynamic character in the novel. Though intelligent, introspective, and sensitive, Denver has been stunted in her emotional growth by years of relative isolation. Beloved's increasing malevolence, however, forces Denver to overcome her fear of the world beyond 124 and seek help from the community. Her foray out into the town and her attempts to find permanent work and possibly attend college mark the beginning of her fight for independence and self-possession.

Beloved—Beloved's identity is mysterious. The novel provides evidence that she could be an ordinary woman traumatized by years of captivity, the ghost of Sethe's mother, or, most convincingly, the embodied spirit of Sethe's murdered daughter. On an allegorical level, Beloved represents the inescapable, horrible past of slavery returned to haunt the present. Her presence, which grows increasingly malevolent and parasitic as the novel progresses, ultimately serves as a catalyst for Sethe's, Paul D's, and Denver's respective processes of emotional growth.

Paul D—The physical and emotional brutality suffered by Paul D at Sweet Home and as part of a chain gang has caused him to bury his feelings in the "rusted tobacco tin" of his heart. He represses his painful memories and believes that the key to survival is not becoming too attached to anything. At the same time, he seems to incite the opening up of others' hearts, and women in particular tend to confide in him. Sethe welcomes him to 124, where he becomes her lover and the object of Denver's and Beloved's jealousy. Though his union with Sethe provides him with stability and allows him to come to terms with his past, Paul D continues to doubt fundamental aspects of his identity, such as the source of his manhood and his value as a person.

Baby Suggs—After Halle buys his mother, Baby Suggs, her freedom, she travels to Cincinnati, where she becomes a source of emotional and spiritual inspiration for the city's black residents. She holds religious gatherings at a place called the Clearing, where she teaches her followers to love their voices, bodies, and minds. However, after Sethe's act of infanticide, Baby Suggs stops preaching and retreats to a sickbed to die. Even so, Baby Suggs continues to be a source of inspiration long after her death: in Part Three her memory motivates Denver to leave 124 and find help. Moreover, it is partially out of respect for Baby Suggs that the community responds to Denver's requests for support.

Stamp Paid—Like Baby Suggs, Stamp Paid is considered by the community to be a figure of salvation, and he is welcomed at every door in town. An agent of the Underground Railroad, he helps Sethe to freedom and later saves Denver's life. A grave sacrifice he made during his enslavement has caused him to consider his emotional and moral debts to be paid off for the rest of his life, which is why he decided to rename himself "Stamp Paid." Yet by the end of the book he realizes that he may still owe protection and care to the residents of 124. Angered by the community's neglect of Sethe, Denver, and Paul D, Stamp begins to question the nature of a community's obligations to its members.

Schoolteacher—Following Mr. Garner's death, schoolteacher takes charge of Sweet Home. Cold, sadistic, and vehemently racist, schoolteacher replaces what he views as Garner's too-soft approach with an oppressive regime of rigid rules and punishment on the plantation. Schoolteacher's own habits are extremely ascetic: he eats little, sleeps less, and works hard. His most insidious form of oppression is his "scientific" scrutiny of the slaves, which involves asking questions, taking physical measurements, and teaching lessons to his white pupils on the slaves' "animal characteristics." The lower-case *s* of schoolteacher's appellation may have an ironic meaning: although he enjoys a position of extreme power over the slaves, they attribute no worth to him.

Halle—Sethe's husband and Baby Suggs's son, Halle is generous, kind, and sincere. He is very much alert to the hypocrisies of the Garners' "benevolent" form of slaveholding. Halle eventually goes mad, presumably after witnessing schoolteacher's nephews' violation of Sethe.

Lady Jones—Lady Jones, a light-skinned black woman who loathes her blond hair, is convinced that everyone despises her for being a woman of mixed race. Despite her feelings of alienation, she maintains a strong sense of community obligation and teaches the underprivileged children of Cincinnati in her home. She is skeptical of the supernatural dimensions of Denver's plea for assistance, but she nevertheless helps to organize the community's delivery of food to Sethe's plagued household.

Ella—Ella worked with Stamp Paid on the Underground Railroad. Traumatized by the sexual brutality of a white father and son who once held her captive, she believes, like Sethe, that the past is best left buried. When it surfaces in the form of Beloved, Ella organizes the women of the community to exorcise Beloved from 124.

Mr. and Mrs. Garner—Mr. and Mrs. Garner are the comparatively benevolent owners of Sweet Home. The events at Sweet Home reveal, however, that the idea of benevolent slavery is a contradiction in terms. The Garners' paternalism and condescension are simply watered-down versions of schoolteacher's vicious racism.

Mr. and Miss Bodwin—Siblings Mr. and Miss Bodwin are white abolitionists who have played an active role in winning Sethe's freedom. Yet there is something disconcerting about the Bodwins' politics. Mr. Bodwin longs a little too eagerly for the "heady days" of abolitionism, and Miss Bodwin demonstrates a condescending desire to "experiment" on Denver by sending her to Oberlin College. The distasteful figurine Denver sees in the Bodwins' house, portraying a slave and displaying the message "At Yo' Service," marks the limits and ironies of white involvement in the struggle for racial equality. Nevertheless, the siblings are motivated by good intentions, believing that "human life is holy, all of it."

Amy Denver—A nurturing and compassionate girl who works as an indentured servant, Amy is young, flighty, talkative, and idealistic. She helps Sethe when she is ill during her escape from Sweet Home, and when she sees Sethe's wounds from being whipped, Amy says that they resemble a tree. She later delivers baby Denver, whom Sethe names after her.

Paul A, Paul F, and Sixo—Paul A and Paul F are the brothers of Paul D. They were slaves at Sweet Home with him, Halle, Sethe, and, earlier, Baby Suggs. Sixo is another fellow slave. Sixo and Paul A die during the escape from the plantation.

ANALYSIS OF MAJOR CHARACTERS

SETHE

Sethe, the protagonist of the novel, is a proud and noble woman. She insists on sewing a proper wedding dress for the first night she spends with Halle, and she finds schoolteacher's lesson on her "animal characteristics" more debilitating than his nephews' sexual and physical abuse. Although the community's shunning of Sethe and Baby Suggs for thinking too highly of themselves is unfair, the fact that Sethe prefers to steal food from the restaurant where she works rather than wait on line with the rest of the black community shows that she does consider herself different from the rest of the blacks in her neighborhood. Yet, Sethe is not too proud to accept support from others in every instance. Despite her independence (and her distrust of men), she welcomes Paul D and the companionship he offers.

Sethe's most striking characteristic, however, is her devotion to her children. Unwilling to relinquish her children to the physical, emotional, and spiritual trauma she has endured as a slave, she tries to murder them in an act that is, in her mind, one of motherly love and protection. Her memories of this cruel act and of the brutality she herself suffered as a slave infuse her everyday life and lead her to contend that past trauma can never really be eradicated—it continues, somehow, to exist in the present. She thus spends her life attempting to avoid encounters with her past. Perhaps Sethe's fear of the past is what leads her to ignore the overwhelming evidence that Beloved is the reincarnation of her murdered daughter. Indeed, even after she acknowledges Beloved's identity, Sethe shows herself to be still enslaved by the past, because she quickly succumbs to Beloved's demands and allows herself to be consumed by Beloved. Only when Sethe learns to confront the past head-on, to assert herself in its presence, can she extricate herself from its oppressive power and begin to live freely, peacefully, and responsibly in the present.

DENVER

Sethe's daughter Denver is the most dynamic character in the novel. She is shy, intelligent, introspective, sensitive, and inclined to spend hours alone in her "emerald closet," a sylvan space formed by boxwood bushes. Her mother considers Denver a "charmed" child who has miraculously survived, and throughout the book Denver is in close contact with the supernatural.

Despite Denver's abilities to cope, she has been stunted emotionally by years of relative isolation. Though eighteen years old, she acts much younger, maintaining an intense fear of the world outside 124 and a perilously fragile sense of self. Indeed, her self-conception remains so tentative that she feels slighted by the idea of a world that does not include her—even the world of slavery at Sweet Home. Denver defines her identity in relation to Sethe. She also defines herself in relation to her sister—first in the form of the baby ghost, then in the form of Beloved. When she feels that she is being excluded from her family's attentions—for example, when her mother devotes her energies to Paul D—Denver feels threatened and angry. Correspondingly, she treats Paul D coldly much of the time.

In the face of Beloved's escalating malevolence and her mother's submissiveness, Denver is forced to step outside the world of 124. Filled with a sense of duty, purpose, and courage, she enlists the help of the community and cares for her increasingly self-involved mother and sister. She enters a series of lessons with Miss Bodwin and considers attending Oberlin College someday. Her last conversation with Paul D underscores her newfound maturity: she presents herself with more civility and sincerity than in the past and asserts that she now has her own opinions.

BELOVED

Beloved's elusive, complex identity is central to our understanding of the novel. She may, as Sethe originally believes, be an ordinary woman who was locked up by a white man and never let out of doors. Her limited linguistic ability, neediness, baby-soft skin, and emotional instability could all be explained by a lifetime spent in captivity. But these traits could also support the theory that is held by most of the characters in the novel, as well as most readers: Beloved is the embodied spirit of Sethe's dead daughter. Beloved is the age the baby would have been had it lived, and she bears the name printed on the baby's tombstone. She first appears to Sethe soaking wet, as though newly born, and Sethe has the sensation of her water breaking when she sees her. Additionally, Beloved knows about a pair of earrings Sethe possessed long ago, she hums a song Sethe made up for her children, she has a long scar under her chin where her death-wound would have been dealt, and her breath smells like milk.

A third interpretation views Beloved as a representation of Sethe's dead mother. In Chapter 22, Beloved recounts memories that correspond to those that Sethe's mother might have had of her passage to America from Africa. Beloved has a strange manner of speaking and seems to wear a perpetual smile—traits we are told were shared by Sethe's mother. By Chapter 26, Beloved and Sethe have switched places, with Beloved acting as the mother and Sethe as the child. Their role reversal may simply mark more explicitly what has been Beloved's role all along. On a more general level, Beloved may also stand for all of the slaves who made the passage across the Atlantic. She may give voice to and embody the collective unconscious of all those oppressed by slavery's history and legacy.

Beloved is presented as an allegorical figure. Whether she is Sethe's daughter, Sethe's mother, or a representative of all of slavery's victims, Beloved represents the past returned to haunt the present. The characters' confrontations with Beloved and, consequently, their pasts, are complex. The interaction between Beloved and Sethe is given particular attention in the book. Once Sethe reciprocates Beloved's violent passion for her, the two become locked in a destructive, exclusive, parasitic relationship. When she is with Beloved, Sethe is paralyzed in the past. She devotes all her attention to making Beloved understand why she reacted to schoolteacher's arrival the way she did. Paradoxically, Beloved's presence is enabling at the same time that it is destructive. Beloved allows and inspires Sethe to tell the stories she never tells—stories about her own feelings of abandonment by her mother, about the harshest indignities she suffered at Sweet Home, and about her motivations for murdering her daughter. By engaging with her past, Sethe begins to learn about herself and the extent of her ability to live in the present.

Beloved also inspires the growth of other characters in the novel. Though Paul D's hatred for Beloved never ceases, their strange, dream-like sexual encounters open the lid of his "tobacco tin" heart, allowing him to remember, feel, and love again. Denver benefits the most from Beloved's presence, though indirectly. At first she feels an intense dependence on Beloved, convinced that in Beloved's absence she has no "self" of her own. Later, however, Beloved's increasingly malevolent, temperamental, self-centered actions alert Denver to the dangers of the past Beloved represents. Ultimately, Beloved's tyranny over Sethe forces Denver to leave 124 and seek help in the community. Denver's exile from 124 marks the beginning of her social integration and of her search for independence and self-possession.

Although Beloved vanishes at the end of the book, she is never really gone—her dress and her story, forgotten by the town but preserved by the novel, remain. Beloved represents a destructive and painful past, but she also signals the possibility of a brighter future. She gives the people of 124, and eventually the entire community, a chance to engage with the memories they have suppressed. Through confrontation, the community can reclaim and learn from its forgotten and ignored memories.

THEMES, MOTIFS, AND SYMBOLS

Themes

Themes are the fundamental and often universal ideas explored in a literary work.

Slavery's Destruction of Identity

Beloved explores the physical, emotional, and spiritual devastation wrought by slavery, a devastation that continues to haunt those characters who are former slaves even in freedom. The most dangerous of slavery's effects is its negative impact on the former slaves' senses of self, and the novel contains multiple examples of self-alienation. Paul D, for instance, is so alienated from himself that at one point he cannot tell whether the screaming he hears is his own or someone else's. Slaves were told they were subhuman and were traded as commodities whose worth could be expressed in dollars. Consequently, Paul D is very insecure about whether or not he could possibly be a real "man," and he frequently wonders about his value as a person.

Sethe, also, was treated as a subhuman. She once walked in on schoolteacher giving his pupils a lesson on her "animal characteristics." She, too, seems to be alienated from herself and filled with self-loathing. Thus, she sees the best part of herself as her children. Yet her children also have volatile, unstable identities. Denver conflates her identity with Beloved's, and Beloved feels herself actually beginning to physically disintegrate. Slavery has also limited Baby Suggs's self-conception by shattering her family and denying her the opportunity to be a true wife, sister, daughter, or loving mother.

As a result of their inability to believe in their own existences, both Baby Suggs and Paul D become depressed and tired. Baby Suggs's fatigue is spiritual, while Paul D's is emotional. While a slave, Paul D developed self-defeating coping strategies to protect him from the emotional pain he was forced to endure. Any feelings he had were locked away in the rusted "tobacco tin" of his heart, and he concluded that one should love nothing too intensely. Other slaves—Jackson Till, Aunt Phyllis, and Halle—went insane and thus suffered a complete loss of self. Sethe fears that she, too, will end her days in madness. Indeed, she does prove to be mad when she kills her own daughter. Yet Sethe's act of infanticide illuminates the perverse forces of the institution of slavery: under slavery, a mother best expresses her love for her children by murdering them and thus protecting them from the more gradual destruction wrought by slavery.

Stamp Paid muses that slavery's negative consequences are not limited to the slaves: he notes that slavery causes whites to become "changed and altered . . . made . . . bloody, silly, worse than they ever wanted to be." The insidious effects of the institution affect not only the identities of its black victims but those of the whites who perpetrate it and the collective identity of Americans. Where slavery exists, everyone suffers a loss of humanity and compassion. For this reason, Morrison suggests that our nation's identity, like the novel's characters, must be healed. America's future depends on its understanding of the past: just as Sethe must come to terms with her past before she can secure a future with Denver and Paul D, before we can address slavery's legacy in the contemporary problems of racial discrimination and discord, we must confront the dark and hidden corners of our history. Crucially, in *Beloved,* we learn about the history and legacy of slavery not from schoolteacher's or even from the Bodwins' point of view but rather from Sethe's, Paul D's, Stamp Paid's, and Baby Suggs's. Morrison writes history with the voices of a people historically denied the power of language, and *Beloved* recuperates a history that had been lost—either due to willed forgetfulness (as in Sethe's repression of her memories) or to forced silence (as in the case of Paul D's iron bit).

The Importance of Community Solidarity

Beloved demonstrates the extent to which individuals need the support of their communities in order to survive. Sethe first begins to develop her sense of self during her twenty-eight days of freedom, when she becomes a part of the Cincinnati community. Similarly, Denver discovers herself and grows up when she leaves 124 and becomes a part of society. Paul D and his fellow prison inmates in Georgia prove able to escape only by working together. They are literally chained to one another, and

Paul D recalls that "if one lost, all lost." Lastly, it is the community that saves Sethe from mistakenly killing Mr. Bodwin and casting the shadow of another sin across her and her family's life.

Cincinnati's black community plays a pivotal role in the events of 124. The community's failure to alert Sethe to schoolteacher's approach implicates it in the death of Sethe's daughter. Baby Suggs feels the slight as a grave betrayal from which she never fully recovers. At the end of the novel, the black community makes up for its past misbehavior by gathering at 124 to collectively exorcise Beloved. By driving Beloved away, the community secures Sethe's, and its own, release from the past.

The Powers and Limits of Language

When Sixo turns schoolteacher's reasoning around to justify having broken the rules, schoolteacher whips him to demonstrate that "definitions belong to the definers," not to the defined. The slaves eventually come to realize the illegitimacy of many of the white definitions. Mr. Garner, for example, claims to have allowed his slaves to live as "real men," but Paul D questions just how manly they actually are. So, too, does Paul D finally come to realize with bitter irony the fallacy of the name "Sweet Home." Although Sixo eventually reacts to the hypocrisy of the rhetoric of slavery by abandoning English altogether, other characters use English to redefine the world on their own terms. Baby Suggs and Stamp Paid, for example, rename themselves. *Beloved* may be read as Morrison's effort to transform those who have always been the defined into the definers.

While slaves, the characters manipulate language and transcend its standard limits. Their command of language allows them to adjust its meanings and to make themselves indecipherable to the white slave owners who watch them. For example, Paul D and the Georgia prison inmates sing together about their dreams and memories by "garbling . . . [and] tricking the words."

The title of the novel alludes to what is ultimately the product of a linguistic misunderstanding. At her daughter's funeral, Sethe interpreted the minister's address to the "Dearly Beloved" as referring to the *dead* rather than the living. All literature is indebted to this "slippery," shifting quality of language: the power of metaphor, simile, metonymy, irony, and wordplay all result from the ability of words to attach and detach themselves from various possible meanings.

MOTIFS

Motifs are recurring structures, contrasts, or literary devices that can help to develop and inform the text's major themes.

The Supernatural

Morrison enhances the world of *Beloved* by investing it with a supernatural dimension. While it is possible to interpret the book's paranormal phenomena within a realist framework, many events in the novel—most notably, the presence of a ghost—push the limits of ordinary understanding. Moreover, the characters in *Beloved* do not hesitate to believe in the supernatural status of these events. For them, poltergeists, premonitions, and hallucinations are ways of understanding the significance of the world around them. Such occurrences stand in marked contrast to schoolteacher's perverse hyper-"scientific" and empirical studies.

Allusions to Christianity

Beloved's epigraph, which is taken from Romans 9:25, bespeaks the presence that Christian ideas will have in the novel. The "four horsemen" who come for Sethe reference the description of the Apocalypse found in the Book of Revelations. Beloved is reborn into Sethe's world drenched with a sort of baptismal water. As an infant, Denver drinks her sister's blood along with her mother's breast milk, which can be interpreted as an act of Communion that links Denver and Beloved and that highlights the sacrificial aspect of the baby's death. Additionally, Sethe's act so horrifies schoolteacher that he leaves without taking her other children, thus allowing them to live in freedom. In this way, the baby's sacrificial death, like that of Christ, brings salvation. The book's larger discussions of sin, sacrifice, redemption, forgiveness, love, and resurrection similarly resound with biblical references.

SYMBOLS

Symbols are objects, characters, figures, or colors used to represent abstract ideas or concepts.

The Color Red

Colors from the red part of the spectrum (including orange and pink) recur throughout *Beloved,* although the meaning of these red objects varies. Amy Denver's red velvet, for example, is an image of hope and a brighter future, while Paul D's "red heart" represents feeling and emotion. Overall, red seems to connote vitality and the visceral nature of human existence. Yet, in *Beloved,* vitality often goes hand in hand with mortality, and red images simultaneously refer to life and death, to presence and absence. For example, the red roses that line the road to the carnival serve to herald the carnival's arrival in town and announce the beginning of Sethe, Denver, and Paul D's new life together; yet they also stink of death. The red rooster signifies manhood to Paul D, but it is a manhood that Paul D himself has been denied. The story of Amy's search for carmine velvet seems especially poignant because we sense the futility of her dream. Sethe's memory is awash with the red of her daughter's blood and the pink mineral of her gravestone, both of which have been bought at a dear price.

Trees

In the world of *Beloved,* trees serve primarily as sources of healing, comfort, and life. Denver's "emerald closet" of boxwood bushes functions as a place of solitude and repose for her. The beautiful trees of Sweet Home mask the true horror of the plantation in Sethe's memory. Paul D finds his freedom by following flowering trees to the North, and Sethe finds hers by escaping through a forest. By imagining the scars on Sethe's back as a "chokecherry tree," Amy Denver sublimates a site of trauma and brutality into one of beauty and growth. But as the sites of lynchings and of Sixo's death by burning, however, trees reveal a connection with a darker side of humanity as well.

The Tin Tobacco Box

Paul D describes his heart as a "tin tobacco box." After his traumatizing experiences at Sweet Home and, especially, at the prison camp in Alfred,

Georgia, he locks away his feelings and memories in this "box," which has, by the time Paul D arrives at 124, "rusted" over completely. By alienating himself from his emotions, Paul D hopes to preserve himself from further psychological damage. In order to secure this protection, however, Paul D sacrifices much of his humanity by foregoing feeling and gives up much of his selfhood by repressing his memories. Although Paul D is convinced that nothing can pry the lid of his box open, his strange, dreamlike sexual encounter with Beloved—perhaps a symbol of an encounter with his past—causes the box to burst and his heart once again to glow red.

SUMMARY AND ANALYSIS

Part One: Chapter 1

Note: The text of Beloved *is divided into Parts One, Two, and Three. Within each part, there are many smaller sections. They function and look like chapters, but are never designated as such by the book itself. For ease of reference, this SparkNote has labeled these sections as numbered chapters. This numbering system runs continuously through all three of the book's parts.*

Summary

124 was spiteful. Full of a baby's venom.

The novel opens in 1873 in Cincinnati, Ohio. For the past eighteen years, Sethe, an ex-slave, and her daughter, Denver, have been living in a house that is haunted by the ghost of Sethe's firstborn baby daughter. Until eight years ago, Sethe's mother-in-law, Baby Suggs, also lived with them in their house at 124 Bluestone Road. Before she died, Baby Suggs sank into a deep depression, exhausted by a life of slavery and by the loss of all eight of her children. She spent her last days requesting "color"—bits of brightly colored objects she hoped would alleviate her sadness. Her death came only a short while after Sethe's sons, Howard and Buglar, each ran away from 124 following encounters with their dead sister's ghost.

Sethe works hard to remember as little as possible about her past, and consequently the memory of her sons is fading fast. Most of her painful memories involve Sweet Home, a plantation in Kentucky where she lived as a slave until her escape eighteen years ago. On this day, however, she returns home and finds an unexpected and surprising guest: Paul D. Paul D was one of five men who were Sethe's fellow slaves at Sweet Home; these had included Paul A, Paul F, Sixo, and Sethe's husband, Halle. Although Sethe hasn't seen Paul D in eighteen years, they slip into easy conversation and Sethe invites him inside. Paul D walks into a pool of eerie red light and feels a wave of grief come over him.

Sethe explains that the presence is the sad specter of her dead baby, whose throat, we have learned, was cut before it was two years old. At her daughter's funeral, Sethe mistook the preacher's reference to the "Dearly Beloved" mourners for a reference to her dead daughter. Afterward, she agreed to ten minutes of sex with an engraver in order to have the word "Beloved" carved on the baby's headstone.

Paul D has desired Sethe ever since she arrived at Sweet Home at the age of thirteen to replace Baby Suggs. Baby Suggs left because her son Halle had bought her freedom with five years of weekend labor. Sethe was beautiful then, and the five male Sweet Home slaves waited in agonizing sexual frustration, having sex with calves and dreaming of rape, while she took a year to make her choice among them. She chose Halle, and together they had two sons and a daughter. Sethe was pregnant with a fourth child, Denver, when the family made its escape from Sweet Home. Sethe and Halle were separated during their escape, however, and neither Paul D nor Sethe knows what happened to Halle.

Seeing her mother flirting and talking about Sweet Home with Paul D makes Denver feel lonely and excluded. She reacts with surly jealousy and dissolves into tears at the dinner table one evening. She cries that she cannot stay in the house because the community knows it to be haunted. Consequently, everyone avoids Denver and she has no friends. When Paul D wonders aloud why they haven't moved from 124, Sethe firmly asserts that she will never run away from anything again.

Later, Sethe explains that she was whipped before she ran from Sweet Home to meet Baby Suggs and her children, whom she had sent ahead, in Cincinnati. The white girl who helped deliver Denver said that the resulting scars looked like a chokecherry tree. Sethe cries and says that the men who beat her stole her baby's milk before she ran. Paul D comes up behind her and pulls down the top of her dress. He cradles her breasts in his hands while he kisses each line of her scars. The house immediately begins to lurch and shake as the ghost vents its rage. Paul D shouts and fights with the ghost, chasing it away. Denver resents Paul D's act—the ghost was the only company she had.

Analysis

From the beginning, *Beloved* focuses on the import of memory and history. Sethe struggles daily with the haunting legacy of slavery, in the form of her threatening memories and also in the form of her daughter's aggressive ghost. For Sethe, the present is mostly a struggle to beat back the past, because the memories of her daughter's death and the experiences at Sweet Home are too painful for her to recall consciously. But Sethe's repression is problematic, because the absence of history and memory inhibits the construction of a stable identity. Even Sethe's hard-won freedom is threatened by her inability to confront her prior life. Paul D's arrival gives Sethe the opportunity and the impetus to finally come to terms with her painful life history.

Already in the first chapter, the reader begins to gain a sense of the horrors that have taken place. Like the ghost, the address of the house is also a stubborn reminder of its history. The characters refer to the house by its number, 124. These digits highlight the absence of Sethe's murdered third child. As an institution, slavery necessarily shattered its victims' traditional family structures, or else precluded such structures from ever forming. Slaves were thus deprived of the foundations of any identity apart from their role as servants. Baby Suggs is a woman who never had the chance to be a real mother, daughter, or sister. Later, we learn that neither Sethe nor Paul D knew their parents, and the relatively long, six-year marriage of Halle and Sethe is an anomaly in an institution that would regularly redistribute men and women to different farms as their owners deemed necessary.

The scars on Sethe's back serve as another testament to her disfiguring and dehumanizing years as a slave. Like the ghost, the scars also work as a metaphor for the way that past tragedies affect us psychologically, "haunting" or "scarring" us for life. More specifically, the tree shape formed by the scars might symbolize Sethe's incomplete family tree. It could also symbolize the burden of existence itself, through an allusion to the "tree of knowledge" from which Adam and Eve ate, initiating their mortality and suffering. Sethe's "tree" may also offer insight into the empowering abilities of interpretation. In the same way that the white men are able to justify and increase their power over the slaves by "studying" and interpreting them according to their own whims, Amy's interpretation of Sethe's mass of ugly scars as a "chokecherry tree" transforms a story of pain and oppression into one of survival. In the hands of the right storyteller, Sethe's marks become a poignant and beautiful symbol. When Paul D kisses them, he reinforces this more positive interpretation.

The chapter provides other similar examples of the way that Paul D's presence works to help Sethe reclaim authority over her own past. Sethe has always prioritized others' needs over her own. For example, although she seems to suggest in her story that schoolteacher's nephews raped her, Sethe is preoccupied with their theft of her breast milk, which shows that she privileges her children's needs over her own. When Paul D cradles her breasts, Sethe is "relieved of their weight." The narrator comments that the "responsibility for her breasts," the symbols of her devotion to her children, was Paul's for a moment. Usually defined by her motherhood, Sethe has a chance to be herself for a moment, whomever that may be. Paul D reacquaints Sethe with her body as a locus for her own desires and not only as a site for the desires of others—whether those of the rapists or those of her babies.

Paul D's arrival is not comforting to Denver because Paul D threatens Denver's exclusive hold on Sethe's affections. He also reminds Denver about the existence of a part of Sethe that she has never been able to access. Although she is eighteen years old, Denver's fragile sense of self cannot bear talk of a world that does not include her. She has lived in relative isolation for her entire life, and she is angered and disturbed by Paul D's sudden intrusion.

The events of the novel unfold on two different temporal planes: the present of Cincinnati in 1873, and Sethe's time at Sweet Home during the 1850s, which is narrated largely in flashback. In this first chapter, Morrison plants the seeds of the major events that will unfurl over the course of the novel: Sethe's encounter with schoolteacher and his nephews; the slaves' escape from Sweet Home; the story of Amy Denver; and the mystery of Sethe's baby's murder. These past events are told in a nonlinear manner, fading and resurfacing cyclically as the characters' memories reveal more and more to the reader and to the characters themselves.

Part One: Chapters 2–3

Summary

Chapter 2

After twenty-five years of fantasizing about Sethe, Paul D finds the consummation of his desire to be a disappointment. He lies awake in Sethe's bed and decides that her "tree" is nothing but an ugly clump of scars. His thoughts turn to Sixo, a fellow slave at Sweet Home, who would walk thirty miles to meet his girlfriend while Halle and the Paul brothers pined away after Sethe.

We learn that although Baby Suggs had eight children by six different men, Halle, her youngest, was the only one who wasn't taken from her. When Halle bought Baby Suggs her freedom, she believed that, at her age, she was too old for her freedom to mean anything.

Paul D's interested gaze reminds Sethe of Halle, whose love was more like that of a brother than that of a man "laying claim." Sethe remembers that when she and Halle first decided to get married, she asked Mrs. Garner if they were to have a wedding, but the white woman only laughed. With nothing to make the partnership official in any way, Sethe secretly stitched herself a dress to mark the occasion. The lovers consummated their relationship in a cornfield, and the swaying corn stalks alerted the other men that Sethe had finally made her choice. That night, the other Sweet Home men ate the fresh corn that came from the stalks broken by Sethe and Halle.

Chapter 3

> *. . . if you go there—you who was never there—if you go there and stand in the place where it was, it will happen again; it will be there . . . it's going to always be there waiting for you.*

Denver turns to the outdoors for comfort and contemplation. Since childhood, she has sought privacy and repose in what she calls her "emerald closet"—a bower formed by a ring of boxwood bushes that smells of cologne she once spilled there. One time, as she was returning from the bower, through the window Denver saw Sethe kneeling in prayer in Baby Suggs's room. A ghostly white dress knelt beside Sethe with its arm around her waist. Denver interpreted the vision as a sign that the baby ghost had "plans." Paul D, she thinks resentfully, has now interrupted those plans.

When Denver had asked her mother what she was praying about, Sethe told her she was thinking about time, memory, and the past. In Sethe's philosophy, "nothing ever dies." This means that past events continue to occur, not only in one's "rememory" but also somehow in the real world. Sethe believes it is possible to "bump into" past events and places again, and her main priority is shielding Denver from these tangible, painful collisions with the past.

Sethe ran away from Sweet Home when she was pregnant with Denver. Sethe's feet had become raw lumps of flesh by the time she collapsed in the woods, where she was found by a white girl, Amy Denver. Amy explained that she had just completed a childhood of indentured servitude and was heading to Boston to get some "carmine" velvet. Carmine, Amy explained, is what people who buy velvet in Boston call "red." When Amy asked Sethe her name, Sethe told her a false name, "Lu." If Sethe were caught, she could be sent back to Sweet Home. Amy led Sethe to an abandoned lean-to and massaged her tortured feet back to life. Sethe later gave birth to her baby with Amy's help, naming the child after the compassionate girl. Because the story is about her birth, Denver loves to hear it told.

After the episode in which Denver believed she saw the baby ghost kneeling next to her praying mother, Sethe told Denver about schoolteacher, who was Mrs. Garner's brother-in-law. After Mr. Garner died, schoolteacher came with his two nephews to run the farm. Schoolteacher used to record his observations of the slaves in a notebook. He prodded them with strange questions, and Sethe believes that the questions broke Sixo's spirit permanently.

As Paul D repairs the furniture he damaged during his confrontation with the ghost, he sings songs he learned while in a chain gang in Alfred, Georgia. After his traumatizing prison experience there, we read, he shut down a large part of his heart and head, operating only on the part that helped him "walk, eat, sleep, sing." The experience of seeing Sethe again begins to reopen the locked part of his mind, and he decides to stay at 124.

Sethe tells Paul D that after her escape, schoolteacher came to Cincinnati to take her and her children back to Sweet Home. Sethe went to jail instead and took Denver with her. Paul D does not ask her for more details because the mention of jail reminds him of his experiences in Alfred. Paul D's decision to stay gives Sethe hope for the future.

Analysis

Chapter 3 begins with Paul D gazing at Sethe's back and it ends with her gazing at his. These images symbolize what is taking place thematically in the chapter: the characters' charting of their respective memories, of what lies behind them, at their backs. Sethe's back also contains the visible scars of her whipping. The narration alternates between two time periods—the present in Cincinnati and the Sweet Home past. The Sweet Home past is presented from both Paul D's and Sethe's perspectives, as the narrator's focus shifts between the two characters. In this way, the novel maps out the points of proximity and distance between them. Both characters, for example, are disappointed after having sex, and they simultaneously begin thinking about Sethe and Halle's encounter in the cornfield twenty-five years ago. On the other hand, Paul D's sudden, secret revulsion toward Sethe's scars suggests an emotional distance that takes even him by surprise.

Sethe recalls that Halle loved her in a brotherly way, not like a man "laying claim." However, beneath the surface of this seemingly positive memory is the fact of the impotence inherent to the slave condition. Even if he had wanted to do so, Halle could not have laid claim to his enslaved wife any more than she could lay claim to herself. Slaves were not permitted to become legally married because marriage means giving yourself in contract to one another, and slaves are already contracted to their owners. The prohibition of marriage also prevented the slaves from having a strong claim on their children. Baby Suggs's loss of her eight children was nothing unusual in slave life. The names of Paul D and his brothers are also a testament to the slaves' lack of ownership over themselves and their children. Paul D's brothers are named Paul A and Paul F, suggesting their interchangeability in the minds of their owners. Moreover, the brothers' last name—Garner—is that of their owner. It thus marks them as the property of another.

Sethe doesn't feel that she can lay claim even to her own memories. She attributes to them certain powers of autonomy, and her explanation to Denver of her concept of time reveals the powerful hold that the past has on her. Sethe regards the past as a malevolent presence that defies even death. Indeed, the past has damaged Sethe and Paul D to such a degree that they wonder if it is even possible to begin putting the pieces back together. Paradoxically, Sethe tries to shelter Denver from the past by isolating her in a house plagued by the ghost of Denver's dead sister.

In contrast, Denver will not flee the past, because she ardently desires a history. This is evident in her obsessive need to reconstruct the events of her birth in as much detail as possible. She longs for the sense of self that history provides. Similarly, her isolation from the rest of the black community impedes the formation of her identity.

Denver's attachment to her "emerald closet" is part of the novel's broader symbolic network of trees and tree images. For Denver, trees provide comfort and shelter. Elsewhere, however, the ability of trees to function as centers of solace and peace is complicated by the way white men have perverted their natural function. Schoolteacher's men bind, burn, and shoot Sixo near the very trees that he and Paul D found trusting and inviting. And while trees bear the blossoms that lead Paul D to freedom in Chapter 10, they also bear the lynching victims that haunt Sethe's memory. It is understandable that Paul D regards Sethe's scar-tissue "tree" with bitter irony. Since white men have reimagined trees as sites of ugliness and brutality, thinks Paul D, Sethe cannot mask the ugliness and brutality of her wounds by seeing her scars as a tree.

PART ONE: CHAPTERS 4–6

Summary

Chapter 4

Denver hurts Paul D by asking him how long he plans to "hang around." Sethe is mortified by Denver's behavior but refuses to allow Paul D to criticize her daughter. Paul D interprets this as a sign of intense motherly love and thinks it is dangerous for an ex-slave to love anything too much. Paul D has learned to love the individuals in his life only partially, so that he has enough love left over for the next person when the first is taken away.

Paul D promises Sethe that she can safely reenter her past because he will be there to catch her if she falls. He invites Denver and Sethe to a carnival in town that is having a special day for blacks. At the carnival, Denver surprises herself by having a good time. The people they see there greet her casually, rather than showing her the contempt she expects. Because he is such an extrovert and so shamelessly thrilled by the carnival, Paul D is a hit with the other carnival-goers. He thus helps reintegrate Sethe and Denver into the community, and he makes a few acquaintances. He also inquires about getting a job. Paul D is amused by the spectacle of the supposed "Wild African Savage," because he says he knew the man back in Roanoke. On the way to and from the carnival, the smell of rotting roses is overpowering. Also, both on the way there and on the way back, Sethe notices that the three shadows of Paul D, Denver, and herself overlap so as to appear to be holding hands. She interprets this as a promising sign that signals future happiness.

Chapter 5

The narrator describes a fully dressed woman walking out of a stream and falling asleep beneath a mulberry tree. The woman moves to a tree stump near the steps of 124, where Paul D, Sethe, and Denver find her as they return from the carnival. Sethe suddenly feels a strange, irrepressible need to urinate and is reminded of her water breaking before Denver's birth. Denver and Paul D take the woman inside, where she drinks cup after cup of water. Her name, it turns out, is Beloved. Her skin is as smooth as a baby's, and she has no recollection of the past. Denver notes that Here Boy, the dog that was disfigured during one of the baby ghost's rages, has disappeared.

Beloved sleeps for four days, waking only to ask for water. While Beloved sleeps, Denver cares for her with a possessive devotion. Beloved's presence makes Paul D uneasy. He remarks that although she acts and sounds sick, she does not show visible signs of ill health—the other day, he tells Sethe, he saw her pick up a rocking chair with one hand. He claims that Denver was also watching, but when he asks Denver for confirmation, she denies having seen any such thing.

Chapter 6

Beloved develops a strange attachment to Sethe. Although she usually hates discussing the past, Sethe enjoys pouring stories into Beloved's eager ears. Beloved asks what has happened to what she calls Sethe's "diamonds." Sethe replies that she once owned some crystal earrings given to her by Mrs. Garner for her wedding. She then recounts the story of her haphazard, patchwork wedding dress.

As she watches Sethe arrange Denver's hair, Beloved asks about Sethe's mother. Sethe explains that she rarely saw her. Sethe remembers that her mother once took her aside and showed her a circle and a cross that had been burned into her skin. She said that Sethe could use these marks to identify her body if she died. When Sethe asked to be marked, too, her mother slapped her. Sethe tells the girls that she did not understand why her mother had done this until she had a mark of her own.

Sethe mentions that her mother was hanged, and she is suddenly stunned by the recollection of a disturbing memory that she had forgotten. Sethe ran to her dead mother, but Nan, another slave woman, pulled Sethe away from her mother's body when Sethe tried to search for the mark. Speaking in her mother's long-forgotten language, Nan told Sethe that the two women had come across the sea in the same ship. The white crewmembers had raped them repeatedly, but Sethe's mother "threw away" the children she had by the white men. Sethe was kept because she had a black father, for whom she was named.

Analysis

Although the cheer of the carnival in Chapter 4 is tempered somewhat by the stench of the rotting roses, the chapter ends on a note of optimism that is perhaps unparalleled in the rest of the book. Sethe begins to think that with Paul D there to support her, she may be able to confront her past. There are other beginnings: Denver and Paul D begin to reconcile with each other, Sethe and Denver begin reconciliation with the community, and Paul D begins to feel at home in Cincinnati.

Beloved's mystical arrival in Chapter 5 interrupts the progress that is made in Chapter 4. In the subsequent chapters, the existing relationships in the novel become unhinged, and the characters recombine with unusual force. Beloved seems to be a manifestation of Sethe's infant daughter who was killed. Details linking her to the daughter include her age, her name, her lack of memory, her smooth, "new" skin, Here Boy's disappearance, Sethe's strange sensation of her "water breaking," and Beloved's impossible knowledge of Sethe's earrings. It is never made clear, however, whether Beloved is a reincarnation of the child—an actual living human who is inhabited by the spirit of the dead baby—or simply a ghost. Paul D's observation of Beloved's secret strength suggests that she is capable of the supernatural violence wreaked by the poltergeist before Paul D's arrival.

In their actions, the residents of 124 treat Beloved as they would a human visitor in need. In their thoughts, however, they associate her with the murdered infant. As the story develops, all three forge relationships with her that are governed by these thoughts. Although Beloved appears on the surface to be a woman, she resembles a baby in many ways. She does not walk steadily, her speech is impaired, she does not have full control over her bodily functions, and she sleeps constantly.

Beloved also represents the untrained and undisciplined desire of an infant. Her single-minded fixation on Sethe resembles that of an infant, who is unable to conceive of an identity separate from its mother and who thinks of its mother as its exclusive possession.

Sethe tries desperately to keep the past at bay, but Beloved's arrival demonstrates the difficulty—indeed, the impossibility—of repressing the past. Over the course of the novel, Sethe's confrontation with that past will prove both destructive and productive. This section emphasizes the beneficial aspects of the process: in Beloved's presence, memories surface that help Sethe understand her past and, consequently, herself. For example, in Chapter 6 Beloved inspires Sethe's memory of her mother's hanging to come to the surface. Sethe's story of the hanging marks the first time Denver has ever heard about her mother's mother. Especially poignant is the blank space in Sethe's memory for the forgotten language of her early years. Perhaps Sethe's failure to remember the African language spoken by her mother is a deliberate part of her attempt to repress her memory of her mother. Importantly, the lost language represents the kind of cultural devastation suffered by the slaves. Just as Beloved partially restores that lost cultural history to Sethe along with her personal history, Morrison's novel restores a repressed part of American history to contemporary readers by including the stories and memories of plantation slaves. Later, in Beloved's monologue in Chapter 22, the slaves' ancestors' memories of the Middle Passage, the ocean crossing between Africa and America, are evoked.

Part One: Chapters 7–8

Summary

Chapter 7

> ***He would keep the rest [of what he had to tell Sethe] where it belonged: in that tobacco tin buried in his chest where a red heart used to be.***

Beloved's presence—especially what is described as her "shining" sexuality—disturbs Paul D. He anxiously interrogates her about her past until Sethe, sensing Beloved's agitation, interrupts him. Afterward, Sethe chastises Paul D for pressing Beloved so cruelly, and during their argument Halle's name comes up. Paul D then tells Sethe the reason Halle didn't meet her during the escape as planned. Halle was in the loft of the barn when Sethe was violated by schoolteacher's nephews. Afterward, he found himself unable to leave. When Sethe realizes that Halle saw everything that schoolteacher and his nephews did to her, she is initially furious that he did not intervene. But Paul D explains that Halle was shattered by the experience: afterward, Paul D saw him sitting blankly by a butter churn; he had smeared butter all over his face. At the time, Paul D was ignorant of the events in the barn and thus wondered what had caused this breakdown in Halle. However, Paul D could not physically form the words to ask him because he had an iron bit in his mouth. Outside, Sethe and Paul D discuss the shame of wearing the bit. Paul D says that the worst part of the punishment was seeing the farm's rooster, named Mister, watch him and walk around more freely than himself. It is thoughts like these that Paul D keeps locked within the rusted "tobacco tin" of his heart.

Chapter 8

While Sethe and Paul D sit on the porch, Beloved and Denver dance together inside the house. Denver asks Beloved how she got her name, and Beloved replies that it is her name "in the dark." Denver asks what it is like in the dark place from which Beloved came. Beloved says that when she was there she was small and curled up. It was hot and crowded with lots of other people, and some of them were dead. She describes a bridge and water. When Denver asks her why she came back, Beloved mentions Sethe, saying she wanted to see "her face." Denver feels slighted that she was not the main reason for Beloved's return.

Denver asks Beloved not to tell Sethe who she really is. Beloved becomes angry and tells Denver never to tell her what to do. She reminds Denver that she doesn't need her—Sethe is the one she needs. The two girls sit in uncomfortable silence until Beloved asks Denver to narrate the story of Denver's birth. As Denver watches the way Beloved eagerly drinks in every detail, she is able to envision the story she narrates.

Denver tells Beloved about how Amy Denver found Sethe and discerned the image of a chokecherry tree in Sethe's bleeding scars. After

Amy cleaned the wounds, the two women spent the night in a lean-to shelter. The next morning, Amy helped Sethe limp down to the river, where they found a leaky boat with one oar. It was upon stepping into the boat that Sethe's water broke. It seemed as though the newborn Denver might die, but Amy finally coaxed a whimper out of her. Later that evening, Amy left Sethe waiting by the riverbank for a chance to cross the river to Ohio.

Analysis

Beloved incites the narration of history time and again. Often, she directly questions Denver and Sethe about the past, but Beloved also has an indirect influence, which the scene between Sethe and Paul D illustrates. It is the couple's argument over Beloved that sparks Paul D's revelation of Halle's fate to Sethe.

Once Beloved has kindled the storytelling process, Sethe and Paul D devote their own energies to it, despite the pain that is involved. For as Amy says to Sethe in Chapter 3 about Sethe's throbbing feet, "Anything dead coming back to life hurts." On a certain level, both Sethe and Paul D realize that it is worth the pain to bring their memories back to life, back into the open. In releasing these memories, they themselves can come back to life and live again without fear. Aware of the pain it will cause, Sethe and Paul D nevertheless proceed to fill in the gaps in each other's knowledge of the past. For both characters, forming a coherent identity involves weaving together the fragments of their past into a coherent narrative.

These chapters focus on Paul D's identity in particular. Mr. Garner always bragged that he raised his slaves as "men," and Paul D had always considered himself a man in his own right. But schoolteacher proved to him that his claim to manhood was not inherent and that it depended upon the will of another. After wearing a bit as an animal would, a portion of Paul D's identity was shattered. His relationship with Sethe prompts him to try to find a way to reclaim his humanity, and the process of narration that Beloved inspires proves integral to his attempt.

Beloved also counters the more general forces of silence that recur throughout the novel. According to Sethe and Baby Suggs, one should withhold all talk of the past. Once, when Sethe did speak, she almost lost her life: her report to Mrs. Garner about the theft of her milk caused her to be whipped nearly to death. Because speech is one of the most important differences between humans and animals, white slave owners did everything they could to control the speech of their slaves. Those who rebelled or did not speak with a suitably deferential tone often had their tongues cut out. Thus, the mere act of *speaking* about a dehumanizing experience is a way of reclaiming one's humanity.

For slaves and former slaves, such speech often takes the form of song or metaphor. For a long while, Paul D was unable to talk about his degrading experiences, but he could describe them through songs. Sethe uses similar circumlocution when she refers to the violation and beating she suffered using the images of stolen milk and of a chokecherry tree. Stylized expression is historically a means of secretly venting anger or criticizing. Thus, for the oppressed, including slaves, artistic expression becomes a matter of survival, because explicit language could be punished with death.

Paradoxically, although Beloved incites the narratives of others, she remains quite cryptic about her own past. What we do hear of her previous experiences suggests that she may be above all a symbolic figure who represents the history of a people. In her interchange with Denver, Beloved's memories of the "dark place" from which she came can be taken as those of a deceased infant girl, but they also greatly resemble an African woman's memories of the "Middle Passage," the crossing of the Atlantic on the way to America. Beloved recalls dark, hot, cramped quarters, a pile of dead bodies, and water. Additionally, the "bridge" she talks about could be the bridge of a ship. These uncanny images will resurface in Beloved's monologue in Chapter 22.

PART ONE: CHAPTERS 9–11

Summary

Chapter 9

Disturbed by Paul D's information about Halle and missing the soothing presence that Baby Suggs once provided, Sethe seeks comfort in a place called the Clearing. She takes Denver and Beloved with her. Before Baby Suggs fell into a depression, for which Sethe blames herself, the older woman used to preach to the black community of Cincinnati in the

Clearing. She would begin by having the people participate in a cathartic mixture of crying, laughter, and dance, and she would then preach self-love. She would instruct them to love their hands that had been bound, their mouths that had been silenced, and, most of all, their hearts.

Sethe recalls the day she arrived at 124 and met Baby Suggs for the first time. After Denver's birth and Amy Denver's departure, she came across a black man fishing with two boys. The man, Stamp Paid, wrapped Denver in a jacket and poled Sethe across the Ohio. On shore, he left a signal for Ella, another organizer of the Underground Railroad, which alerted her to the presence of a "passenger" who needed help. When Ella arrived, Sethe explained that she was heading to Baby Suggs's house on Bluestone Road. Ella, noting Sethe's attachment to Denver, voiced her opinion that one shouldn't love anything too much.

When Sethe got to 124, Baby Suggs welcomed and bathed her before allowing her to see her two boys and her "crawling already? girl." To amuse her daughter, Sethe jingled the earrings that Mrs. Garner had given her. During the twenty-eight days she spent in Cincinnati before her daughter's death, Sethe enjoyed being a part of the community. In the Clearing, she had felt for the first time as though she owned herself.

As she sits on Baby Suggs's old rock in the Clearing, Sethe calls silently for the calming fingers of her deceased mother-in-law. She begins to feel Baby Suggs massaging her neck, but the touch turns suddenly violent and Sethe realizes she is being strangled. Denver reacts with alarm, and Beloved caresses and kisses the bruises on Sethe's neck. Beloved's breath smells like milk to Sethe, and her touch feels like that of the baby's ghost. Alarmed, Sethe pushes Beloved away, saying, "You too old for that." Later, Denver accuses Beloved of strangling Sethe. Beloved runs away in anger, insisting that Sethe was being choked by the "circle of iron," not by her.

We learn that as a seven-year-old Denver attended school lessons with other black children at the home of a woman they called Lady Jones. Denver had been studying there for a year when her classmate Nelson Lord upset her by asking, "Didn't your mother get locked away for murder?" Denver repeated the question to her mother, but she went "deaf" before she could hear an answer. This deafness was cured by the sound of the baby ghost climbing the stairs. It was the first time the ghost had appeared. But after this first innocuous manifestation, the ghost proceeded to become spiteful, angry, and deliberately abusive. Thinking back to these acts of rage, Denver wonders what havoc Beloved might now wreak on Sethe. Yet she believes she has no power to stop her, especially since she so often feels captivated by the girl. When she goes to Beloved to seek forgiveness for fighting with her, she sees Beloved watching two turtles mate.

Chapter 10

Paul D was sent to prison in Alfred, Georgia, because he tried to kill Brandywine, the man to whom schoolteacher sold him. The prison had forty-six inmates, all of them black men. They were locked in small boxes in the ground at night and were subject to sexual abuse and chain gang work during the day. During this time Paul D began to tremble chronically, and his trembling only subsided when he was actively working and singing in the chain gang. Once, during a long rainstorm, the ground turned to mud, which allowed the prisoners to work together and escape. Linked together with one chain, they walked to a camp of ailing Cherokees, who broke their chains. They directed Paul D northward by telling him that he should follow the blooms of the flowers as the warm spring temperatures spread from south to north. In Delaware he met a weaver woman with whom he proceeded to live for eighteen months. As time went on, he locked all his painful memories of the prison and Sweet Home into "the tobacco tin lodged in his chest."

Chapter 11

At 124 Bluestone Road, Paul D feels inexplicably restless and uncomfortable in every room. Eventually, he is only able to sleep outside the house. He realizes that Beloved is moving him around the house like a rag doll. One night, Beloved comes to Paul D in the cold house, where he now sleeps, and says, "I want you to touch me on the inside part. . . . And you have to call me my name." Paul D tries to resist her strange power, but he has sex with her, and the tin tobacco box breaks open. He repeats the phrase "red heart" over and over.

Analysis

Chapter 9 contrasts two philosophies for dealing with pain. One is represented by Baby Suggs; Paul D and Ella espouse the other strategy.

Through her preaching, Baby Suggs hoped to help her fellow former slaves reclaim themselves, to "love their mouths" and express their feelings. While still in bondage, love was an emotional liability, but outside of slavery a person can have more trust that the object of his or her love will not be taken away. Yet, even when one is no longer a slave, one must deal with a certain amount of loss. Having already known more loss than they feel they can bear, Paul D and Ella have decided they would willingly forego all real love for the rest of their lives rather than feel any more pain. When Baby Suggs tells her listeners to love their *hearts* most of all, she directly responds to Paul D's "tin heart" philosophy. Baby Suggs's message is that a sacrifice such as Paul D's is not worth undertaking, because love is part of being human, and humanity should not be sacrificed for the sake of mere emotional survival. It is questionable whether life without love constitutes "survival" at all.

Sethe's reaction to the news of Halle's fate reveals her strategy for coping with pain and love. She wavers and is tempted to suppress her feelings as Paul D does. Ultimately, though, she supports Baby Suggs's wise words. Having loved Halle so deeply, the news of his psychological breakdown causes Sethe great pain. Yet facing his pain and her own allows her to heal and move on. Instead of moving to a new, unhaunted house, Sethe had stayed at 124 in the hope that her husband would join her someday. As she begins to reexamine the past, Sethe contemplates constructing a new family and life with Paul D. Her decision to stay with him suggests that she is ready to confront the other painful accounts that Paul D still has yet to tell her, and to tell her own stories as well. She has taken another step toward reclaiming her identity and healing her spirit.

Similarly, the sexual encounter between Beloved and Paul D causes Paul D to act against his philosophy, which suggests that it is weak in relation to that of Baby Suggs. Paul D's engagement with Beloved may be representative of the intense encounter with his past that he is undertaking in the novel. Somehow, the encounter loosens the lid of Paul D's "tobacco tin" heart: his pulsating chant, "red heart, red heart," reflects the sudden overflow of passion he feels as his tin box bursts and his past pours out.

The scene between Beloved and Paul D raises many questions. Beloved's sexuality complicates the characters' (and the reader's) perception of her as the embodiment of the dead baby's spirit. Her interaction with Paul D seems to prove her power over him, but it also manifests a more vulnerable, plaintive, childlike aspect of her nature. Her insistence that Paul D call her by her name communicates her insecurity about who she is as well as her neediness. If Beloved is representative of history or the past, her actions seem to suggest that although the past has power over us, it is also in a position of dependency. If we do not care for it, acknowledge it, call it by name, it may fade and weaken, but it may also resort to a state of spiteful vengeance, keeping us captive until we bow to its demands.

PART ONE: CHAPTERS 12–14

Summary

Chapter 12

Denver's attachment to Beloved intensifies. Beloved's gaze sustains and completes Denver, and Denver fears that she has no self apart from Beloved. Meanwhile, Sethe, ignoring her earlier sense that Beloved is her daughter's reincarnation, decides that Beloved must have recently escaped from years of captivity. She knows Ella to have endured such an experience: a white man and his son locked her up and raped her repeatedly.

Denver often feels lonely and rejected by Beloved. When she isn't directly stimulated, Beloved lapses into a dreamy silence, and she never interacts as much with Denver as she does with Sethe. Denver, interested only in the present, does not care for the stories about the past that Sethe narrates in response to Beloved's questions. Denver also knows about Beloved's attentions to Paul D because she has noted her nighttime trips to the cold house where he sleeps.

One day, Denver and Beloved go into the cold house to get cider. Suddenly, Beloved disappears into the darkness. Denver is certain that Beloved has gone forever and begins to cry, only to find Beloved in front of her, smiling. Beloved reassures Denver by telling her, "This the place I am." Beloved then drops to the ground where she curls up and moans softly. Her eyes focus on a spot in the darkness where she claims to see "her face." When Denver asks her to clarify, she says mysteriously, "It's me."

Chapter 13

Thinking about schoolteacher's arrival at Sweet Home makes Paul D again question the legitimacy of his manhood in the way that schoolteacher used to force him to do. He likens Beloved's current manipulation of him to schoolteacher's abuse and decides that the only way he can hope to stop Beloved is to tell Sethe what has been happening. He meets her outside the restaurant where she works, but he cannot muster up enough courage to confess that he is "not a man." He surprises himself—and Sethe, who thinks he is about to tell her he is leaving—by asking her to have a baby with him. It begins to snow, and they laugh and flirt on the walk home. Beloved, who has been waiting for Sethe, meets them outside and absorbs Sethe's attention, leaving Paul D feeling cold and resentful. Sethe, however, breaks Beloved's spell by insisting that Paul D resume sleeping with her at night. Sethe decides she cannot have a baby with Paul D because "[u]nless carefree, motherlove was a killer." She begins to question Paul D's intentions: perhaps, she thinks, he is jealous of Denver and Beloved and wants his own family. Ultimately, Sethe recognizes that she is just trying to justify her decision to not have any more children.

Chapter 14

After Sethe takes Paul D upstairs, Beloved begs Denver to drive Paul D away, but Denver replies that Sethe will be angry at Beloved if Paul D leaves. One of Beloved's teeth falls out, and she wonders fearfully if her entire body will begin to fall apart. She finds it difficult to feel complete and unified when Sethe is away. Beloved begins to cry, and Denver takes her in her arms, while the snow gathering outside 124 piles higher and higher.

Analysis

The language used to describe Denver's relationship with Beloved is loaded with the vocabulary of need and desire. Denver feels that Beloved's interested gaze sends her to a place "beyond appetite" and that looking at Beloved is "food enough." Beloved provides emotional sustenance for Denver in a way that Sethe never could, because Denver is simultaneously responsible for and dependent upon Beloved. Beloved's constant neediness is most like an infant's desire for its mother; when

Sethe is not there for Beloved, Denver becomes a sort of surrogate mother figure. She is forced out of her role as a daughter and into a more adult role that involves working in the interest of another's welfare.

Indeed, both need and desire recur in *Beloved* as forces active in the shaping of human relationships. Indulging desire seems to affirm life. At the same time, repressing desire is self-destructive. Thus, Paul D's attempts to reject his desire for Beloved are ultimately detrimental and inhibit him from constructing a complete identity.

When Beloved curls up into a ball and rocks herself back and forth in the shed, her behavior recalls her description of life in the "other place"—whether womb, grave, or slave ship—where she lay curled up and hot. In this scene, Beloved points to a spot in the darkness where she sees "her face." "Me. It's me," she tells Denver. Beloved may be conflating her identity with Sethe's, possibly because her premature death prevented her from forming an independent sense of self. She could also be pointing to the spot in the shed where she was murdered. Alternatively, if we understand much of Beloved's speech as voicing the thoughts of the slaves during the Middle Passage, her words here may refer not to her own situation but to that of the slaves. Perhaps they refer specifically to the circumstances of her grandmother, Sethe's mother. Thus, when Beloved identifies "her" face with "me," she may be speaking in the voice of Sethe's mother.

Paul D's proposal that he get Sethe pregnant reveals his desire to redirect his attention from the past to the future. He has been worrying about his manhood and has been tormented by the curse Beloved seems to have cast over him. When he surprises himself by telling Sethe that he wants her to have a baby with him, he decides retroactively that a baby would be the perfect "solution: a way to hold on to her, document his manhood and break out of the girl's spell—all in one." But Sethe feels she has already paid too high a price for motherhood. She has already lost three children and does not want to have another, only to see it, too, run away or be taken from her. Sethe further demonstrates her reluctance to engage with her past when she ignores her earlier sense that Beloved is her daughter. Sethe does not feel ready to face up to the horrible fact that she killed her own daughter, a mother's worst crime. Willfully rejecting her own instinct, Sethe convinces herself that Beloved must be an ordinary girl who has escaped from some sort of captivity.

Part One: Chapters 15–18

Summary

Chapter 15

After Sethe first arrived at 124, Stamp Paid brought over two pails of rare, deliciously sweet, blackberries. Baby Suggs decided to bake some pies, and before long the celebration had transformed into a feast for ninety people. The community celebrated long into the night but grew jealous and angry as the feast wore on: to them, the excess of the feast was a measure of Baby Suggs's unwarranted pride. Baby Suggs sensed a "dark and coming thing" in the distance, but the atmosphere of jealousy created by the townspeople clouded her perception.

From Sethe's arrival at 124, the narration goes even further back in time to Sweet Home. Although it meant leaving behind the only child she had been able to see grow to adulthood, Baby Suggs allowed Halle to buy her freedom because it mattered so much to him. Once she left Sweet Home, Baby Suggs realized how sweet freedom could be. While Mr. Garner drove her to Cincinnati, she asked him why he and Mrs. Garner called her Jenny. He told her that Jenny Whitlow was the name on her bill-of-sale. She explains the origin of her real name—Suggs was her husband's name, and he called her "Baby." Mr. Garner tells her that Baby Suggs is "no name for a freed Negro." He takes Baby Suggs to Ohio to meet the Bodwins, two white abolitionist siblings who allow Baby Suggs to live at 124 Bluestone Road in exchange for domestic work. Baby Suggs is unable to learn anything about the whereabouts of her lost children.

Chapter 16

One day, about a month after Sethe arrived at 124, schoolteacher showed up at the house with one of his nephews, the sheriff, and a slave catcher. In the woodshed, they found Sethe's sons, Howard and Buglar, lying in the sawdust, bleeding. Sethe was holding her bleeding "crawling already?" daughter, whose throat she had cut with a saw. Stamp Paid rushed in and grabbed Denver before Sethe succeeded in dashing her brains out against the wall. Because none of the children could ever be of any use as a slave, schoolteacher concluded that there was nothing worth claiming at 124 and left in disgust. Sethe's older daughter was dead, but Baby Suggs bound the boys' wounds and struggled with Sethe over Denver. Denver nursed at Sethe's breast, ingesting her dead sister's blood along with her mother's milk. The sheriff took Sethe, with Denver in her arms, to jail.

Chapter 17

Stamp Paid shows Paul D a newspaper clipping with a drawing of Sethe, but Paul D, refusing to believe that the woman depicted is Sethe, insists, "That ain't her mouth." Paul D can't read, so Stamp Paid tells him the story of Sethe's tragedy. Stamp Paid leaves some parts of the story out, though. He doesn't tell how Sethe grabbed her children and flew with them to the woodshed "like a hawk on the wing," nor does he mention that, out of jealous spite, the community purposefully neglected to warn Sethe about schoolteacher's approach.

Chapter 18

> ***She just flew. Collected every bit of life she had made, all the parts of her that were precious and fine and beautiful, and carried, pushed, dragged them . . . away, over there where no one could hurt them.***

When Paul D confronts Sethe with the newspaper clipping, she begins to circle frantically around the room in a manner that parallels the circular manner in which she unravels her story for him. She tells Paul D how, at 124, she began to love her children with renewed force, because she knew finally that they were fully hers to love. When she recognized schoolteacher's hat outside the house one day, she felt hummingbird wings beating around her head and could think only, "No. No. Nono. Nonono." Killing her children was a way of protecting them from the horrors of slavery she had herself endured, a way to secure their safety.

Paul D tells her that her love is "too thick." He feels distanced from Sethe and condemns her act, saying, "You got two feet, Sethe, not four," by which he suggests that she acted like a beast in attempting to murder her own children. His anxiety increases when he sees Beloved standing on the staircase. He leaves 124, and Sethe simply says, "So long." Although he does not say so, Sethe knows that Paul D isn't coming back.

Analysis

When, after many years of service, Baby Suggs asks the Garners why they call her Jenny Whitlow, she reveals a gap in her self-knowledge. However, this gap is quickly closed and surpassed. By choosing to keep the name she knows as her own despite Mr. Garner's protestations, Baby Suggs closes the gap and asserts her independence. She takes this further in her preaching, as it enables her to spread her messages of self-love and independence to the community. In preaching, Baby Suggs takes her community as her family and finds a sense of purpose to her life as a freed person.

But the community is fickle. Although it allows Baby Suggs to rebuild for herself a sense of belonging, it does great harm to Baby Suggs's family. The community is implicated in the tragedy of the infanticide because their jealousy and mistrust weighs on the feast so palpably that it hinders Baby Suggs's perception of the "dark and coming thing." More obviously incriminating is the fact that, out of spite, the community deliberately fails to warn Sethe of schoolteacher's approach. Even after Sethe murders her daughter, the community members feel Sethe is behaving too proudly, a crime for which they will continue to shun her until Denver turns to them for help in Part Three.

Morrison's indictment of the black community in Sethe's crime exemplifies the moral ambiguity that pervades *Beloved.* Like Baby Suggs, Morrison does not seem to "approve or condemn" Sethe's act. Because Morrison centers the novel's narrative around Sethe, and because she portrays Sethe as strong, sane, courageous, and a loving mother, we tend to sympathize with Sethe—even as she explains the circumstances of the murder. At the other extreme is the community, which completely shuns Sethe and her family after she murders her daughter. Thus, while Paul D's initial, horrified reaction to Stamp Paid's story is justified and understandable, it seems out of place to us because the text locates Sethe's act outside the bounds of ethical evaluation in a way that the community does not. The text shifts the focus of the reader's criticism from Sethe herself to the perverse circumstances that have worked upon her to transform her "too thick" motherly love into infanticide.

The book's moral ambiguity extends beyond its central conflict to all aspects of the story. Good and evil are not split along a racial divide—we see whites performing good acts along with the bad and blacks performing bad acts along with the good. By complexly intertwining virtue and vice, Morrison makes her characters seem realistic and human, so that they rise above being simple allegorical figures. Even Beloved, the only expressly allegorical figure in the book, is a complex and elusive character.

The novel's sole definitive moral judgment is its condemnation of all forms of slavery. Most prominently, the terror and despair slavery represents to Sethe is portrayed as the indirect cause of her act of infanticide. Even the "softer" form of slavery practiced by the Garners does not escape open criticism.

The "four horsemen"—schoolteacher, schoolteacher's nephew, a slave catcher, and the sheriff—reference the description of the Apocalypse that is detailed in the Book of Revelations. In the biblical text, the four horsemen—famine, plague, war, and death—herald the coming of the end of human existence. The horsemen in *Beloved* announce the end of the peaceful world that was 124. Before their arrival, Sethe lived in harmony with her family, with her community, and, for the first time, with herself. After Sethe's attempt to murder all of her children, Baby Suggs sinks into a deep depression and never preaches again, while the community shuns 124 and its inhabitants. Sethe's surviving children will never again trust her in the same way, and Sethe is haunted for the rest of her life—literally by her daughter's ghost, figuratively by her deed. In a sense, schoolteacher and his posse also herald the end of coherent meaning for the book's main characters: Sethe's incomprehensible act ushers in an era of moral and existential doubt in the book. Paul D, who has difficulty understanding his feelings, his motives, his manhood, and his actions, is most explicitly plagued by doubt.

PART TWO: CHAPTER 19

Summary

> *White people believed that . . . under every dark skin was a jungle . . . In a way, [Stamp Paid] thought, they were right . . . But it wasn't the jungle blacks brought with them. . . . It was the jungle whitefolks planted in them. And it grew . . . until it invaded the whites who had made it.*

When Stamp Paid hears that Paul D has left 124, he feels guilty for having told Paul D about Sethe's crime without considering her family's welfare. Stamp Paid reminds himself that he has a duty to Sethe and Denver by virtue of their connection to Baby Suggs, of whom he was very fond. He thinks about her late-life depression, which deeply saddened him. He tried to convince her to continue preaching God's word, but she claimed she had lost all motivation after the white men's intrusion into her household.

For the first time since Baby Suggs's death, Stamp returns to 124. When he approaches the house, he hears a clamor of disturbing, disembodied conversation. He can discern only the word "mine." Although he has a habit of walking into houses without knocking—it is the one privilege he claims in exchange for the good he does for the Cincinnati community—Stamp Paid feels uncomfortable entering 124 unannounced. He stands awkwardly at the door and thinks about what he ought to do.

We read that Sethe takes Beloved and Denver ice-skating, partly to show that she has not been devastated by Paul D's departure. Later, Sethe hears Beloved humming a song Sethe made up to sing to her children. Faced with such evidence, Sethe finally recognizes Beloved as her resurrected daughter. Now that her dead child has rejoined her, she decides to discard the past and the future for the "timeless present" of 124.

After returning to 124 several more times and finding himself unable to knock on each occasion, Stamp Paid finally works up the courage to knock on Sethe's door. No one answers. When he peeks in the window, he sees Denver sleeping in front of the fire, but he does not recognize Beloved and her presence disturbs him. When he asks around about the stranger in Sethe's home, his friend Ella tells him that Paul D is sleeping at the church. Stamp chastises Ella for not offering Paul D a place to stay, and he is angered by the community's general neglect of Paul D and of the women.

Stamp wonders whether perhaps he has made a mistake in staying away from 124 for so long, whether he might not owe something to Baby Suggs's kin. Earlier in his life, he decided that he no longer owed anyone anything. While a slave, Stamp was forced to give his wife to his master's son to sleep with, and he concluded that his wife was a gift so terrible that it freed him forever after of all obligation. For this reason, he changed his name from Joshua to Stamp Paid.

Sethe cooks all morning at a restaurant and then takes her lunch home. Occasionally, she steals food and supplies because she is too proud to endure the local grocer's racism. She feels ashamed of her petty thievery and remembers an occasion when Sixo stole a small pig from Sweet Home. When schoolteacher confronted him, Sixo cleverly talked his way out of blame by insisting that he was actually improving schoolteacher's property by feeding himself so that he could better work the land. Schoolteacher whipped him to teach him that "definitions belonged to the definers—not to the defined."

Sethe's memory of Sixo launches a series of other memories about Sweet Home and slavery. One is so painful that Sethe has told it to no one but Beloved: schoolteacher treated the slaves like farm stock, measuring their body parts and studying them like biological specimens. Once, Sethe overheard him giving a lesson to his nephews about her in which he instructed them to categorize each of her characteristics as either human or animal. Schoolteacher again manifested his cruelty again when, after Baby Suggs's departure, he stopped Halle from doing any more work outside Sweet Home, thus depriving him of the chance to pay for the rest of his family's release from slavery. This incident sparked the family to plot a secret escape. But their plan met with a tragic conclusion: Halle went insane, Paul A was hanged, Sixo was burned, and Paul D ended up with a bit in his mouth. Sethe recalls one night when she and Halle discussed the days of Mr. Garner's rule of Sweet Home, the days before schoolteacher and his sadistic nephews arrived. Halle had surprised Sethe by saying that he saw no real difference between Garner's kind of slavery and schoolteacher's.

When Stamp runs away from 124 without knocking, he believes that the "undecipherable" voices he hears from the porch of the house belong to the "black and angry dead." The chapter ends with Stamp's thoughts about how slavery dehumanizes everyone involved, including whites. By defining the blacks as "jungle"-like, the whites "plant" resentment among the blacks that burgeons into a real, "jungle" anger. The whites, in turn, become so frightened of their own creation that they, too, began to behave brutally, like animals. The jungle, Stamp thinks, touches everyone, but it is normally hidden. Only from time to time does it manifest itself in rumblings such as the ones he hears emanating from 124.

Analysis

In this chapter, Stamp Paid's feelings of guilt are interspersed with Sethe's memories of schoolteacher and Sweet Home. The result is a sort of dialogue centering on issues of responsibility and blame. The majority of the black characters in *Beloved* are unhappy, but it is unclear whether the white people are solely responsible or whether the blacks' sorrows are to some extent due to their inability to come to terms with themselves and their pasts. The chapter also raises questions about what the black community owes to itself and about the ties that bind people who are no longer slaves.

The complex, confused dynamics of Beloved's behavior—alternately weak and strong, vulnerable and invincible, loving and malicious, needy and omnipotent—represent the irony and contradiction inherent in Stamp Paid's portrait of the black psyche. Stamp Paid believes that black people feel the need to work extremely hard because they wish to dissociate themselves from white people's image of them as a savage, animalistic species. Yet, Stamp Paid notes, the harder they work to demonstrate their humanity, the more bitter and angry they become. In the end, that rage begins to threaten the very humanity they had been trying to protect and emphasize. In this way, thinks Stamp, the whites succeed in creating a kind of savagery where there was none before, and that savagery in turn spreads to the whites themselves. The result is a snarled and anarchic jungle in which questions of blame and guilt can seem almost impossible to unravel. Stamp Paid's meditation on the tangled network of guilt and retribution that forms racism's "jungle" expands the chapter's focus from individual characters and the local black community to the black community at large.

Although, as his chosen name signifies, Stamp Paid used to believe that his own suffering and deprivation freed him from future obligations, he now begins to realize that it may be his responsibility to look out for Denver's and Sethe's welfare. He also decides that Baby Suggs is to blame for her own depression, which he saw as her surrender to her oppressors. In Stamp's mind, when Baby Suggs decided to stop speaking "the Word," she made a choice to "wear the bit," even though Baby Suggs herself blamed the whites for her suffering and cited the intrusion of the four horsemen as the beginning of her emotional deterioration. Stamp Paid reminds himself that the black community contributed to Baby

Suggs's eventual descent by failing to warn her of schoolteacher's approach, thus hindering her ability to prevent the tragedy. These memories end up muddying his formerly clear-cut understanding of Baby Suggs's plight.

Sethe, too, deals with issues of guilt. Although she tells herself that she does not need to explain to Beloved what led her to murder a daughter because Beloved already understands, Sethe nonetheless continues to detail her motivations mentally, which suggests her need to justify her actions to herself. Sethe has invested all of her identity in motherhood. Every sacrifice she made was for her children and every abuse she suffered she felt as an offense against her children because, in Sethe's eyes, her children are extensions of herself and vice versa. Her behavior—plotting out how to explain her act of infanticide to Beloved and to herself—suggests that however much Sethe blames her murder of Beloved on the oppression of slavery, she in fact places a good deal of the blame for the murder on her own shoulders.

Part Two: Chapters 20–23

Summary

Chapter 20

With Chapter 20, a series of stream-of-consciousness monologues begins. Sethe speaks in this chapter, followed by Denver in Chapter 21 and Beloved in Chapter 22. Chapter 23 comprises a chorus of the three voices. In Chapter 20, Sethe begins, "Beloved, she my daughter. She mine." Sethe wants to explain everything to Beloved so that her daughter will understand why her own mother killed her. Sethe cannot understand why, despite all the clues, she initially failed to recognize that Beloved was her daughter incarnate. She decides Paul D must have distracted her.

Throughout the chapter, Sethe ponders the power of a mother's love. She remembers that her own mother was hanged, but she does not know the circumstances that prompted the lynching. Perhaps her mother attempted to run away, but without Sethe. Sethe wants to believe her mother would never have abandoned her, that she was as devoted a mother as Sethe herself is. After killing Beloved, Sethe wanted to lie down in the grave with her dead daughter. Yet she knew she couldn't give up; she had to keep going for the sake of her three living children.

Chapter 21

Denver's voice emerges in this chapter, which begins, "Beloved is my sister." Denver knows that she swallowed her sister's blood along with her mother's milk. She confesses that she has loved Sethe out of fear, and that Howard and Buglar ran away because they, like Denver, feared that whatever it was that motivated Sethe to kill her children might resurface one day. Denver believes that Beloved returned to help her wait for her father to come home. Denver is also convinced that she must protect Beloved from Sethe. She remembers everything Baby Suggs told her about Halle, which was that he was an angel who loved things too much. The power of his love used to scare Baby Suggs because she knew that the large size of his heart made it an easy target. Denver's youth has been comprised of her fear of her mother and her hope for her father's arrival.

Chapter 22

Beloved's fragmented and complex monologue constitutes the third of the first-person stream-of-consciousness monologues. She begins, "I am Beloved and she is mine." Her patchy memories are of a time when she crouched among dead bodies. She speaks of thirst and hunger, of death and sickness, and of "men without skin." She says all the people are trying to leave their bodies behind.

Beloved then focuses on a woman whose face she "wants" because it is hers. The rest of the monologue consists of Beloved's description of her attempt to "join" with the woman. She wishes she could bite the "iron circle" from around the woman's neck and mentions the woman's "sharp earrings" and "round basket" several times. At the end of the chapter, Beloved is "in the water," and neither she nor the woman has an iron circle around her neck any longer. She is swallowed by the woman and, suddenly, she *is* the woman. She sees herself swim away and says, "I am alone." She then describes emerging from the water and needing to find a place to be. When she opens her eyes, she sees the "face [she] lost." She says that "Sethe's is the face that left [her]." Beloved ends her monologue by saying, "now we can join a hot thing."

Chapter 23

Beloved's words give way to a passage of poetic prose in which the three women's voices come together and mingle, although not in a typical dialogic style. Beloved says that she and Sethe lost and found one another. She tells Sethe that she came back from the other side for her, that she remembers her, and that she is scared the men without skin will come back. Sethe assures her that they will not. Denver warns Beloved not to love Sethe too much. Beloved says she already loves Sethe too much, and Denver promises to protect her. Beloved begs Sethe never to leave her again and Sethe complies. Beloved laments that Sethe left and hurt her.

Analysis

When Stamp Paid hears the unintelligible clamor outside 124 in Chapter 19, the narrator identifies the noise as "the thoughts of the women of 124, unspeakable thoughts, unspoken." In these, the next four chapters, the "unspeakable" and "unspoken" thoughts are finally put into words. Specifically, they are turned into literature through the use of literary devices such as imagery, allusion, and symbol, which are what allow the seemingly "unspeakable" to be verbalized. Indeed, the language in Chapters 20 through 23, which is extremely stylized to represent each character's stream of consciousness, seems to emphasize the fact of its literariness as much as the nature of its message.

As she meditates on her murder of her daughter, Sethe makes mental and emotional connections to her own mother, whom she suspects of having tried to escape without bringing Sethe along. Sethe wants to differentiate her act of infanticide from what she imagines to be her mother's rejection of her. She conceives of her own act as one of love, free of the disregard or contempt that would motivate an abandonment. Moreover, Sethe sees the fact that she protected her children from slavery as a step toward countering her own mother's desertion of her. But Denver's monologue also focuses on family bonds, and her words reveal a previously unarticulated pain at not having grown up in a complete family. She, too, seems to feel abandoned in some sense. More generally, Denver's monologue seems to suggest that even in freedom, the black family as an institution suffers fragmentation and destruction.

The fragmented nature of each of the three monologues is representative of each character's fragmented, incoherent identity. And when their voices mingle in Chapter 23, it is difficult to attribute each phrase to its appropriate speaker. One interpretation of this predicament is that Sethe, Beloved, and Denver have conflated and confused their identities beyond recognition. Beloved cannot cut the psychological umbilical cord that attaches her to Sethe.

Beloved's monologue is highly impressionistic, incredibly dense, and its meaning is elusive. The cramped, dark place that she describes could be a grave full of the "black and angry dead," like the one Stamp Paid perceived to be lingering around 124. It could also be a metaphorical, inescapable womb. The reading the text best seems to support is that Beloved is describing a slave ship transporting Africans to America. For instance, she mentions piled-up corpses. Packed in overcrowded hulls, many Africans died of disease and starvation on the journey to America. Beloved's references to rape echo the experiences of Sethe's mother, who was "taken up many times by the crew" during the Middle Passage. Sea-colored bread refers to the moldy, inedible provisions on board, and the "hot thing" could be a branding iron like the one that marked Sethe's mother. The "men without skin" seem to be the white captors and masters who oppressed the slaves. Thus, Beloved reminds Sethe not only of the crime for which Sethe cannot forgive herself but also functions as a conduit for memories of the history of slavery. Within the novel, the two are certainly presented as interlinked, and Sethe needs to come to terms with both her family's history and the history of slavery.

Of course, literariness in *Beloved* is not limited to these four chapters: as a larger story and work of art, the novel allows its characters, and, more important, their real-life counterparts (the generations of men and women victimized by slavery), to transcend the limits of speech and memory. The book as a whole gives voice to a suppressed history and recovers the memories that the characters themselves—both white and black—try to destroy. Morrison demonstrates literature's ability to recuperate a history that would otherwise be lost to the ravages of willed forgetfulness and silence.

PART TWO: CHAPTERS 24–25

Summary

Chapter 24

Paul D, who has been sleeping in the basement of the local church, is filled with despair. He reflects on his past and notes that his two half brothers, Paul A and Paul F, are the only family he has ever known. He does not remember his mother and never saw his father. Throughout his life, whenever he met large black families living together, he loved to hear them describe to him how they were related. Paul D's thoughts then turn to Mr. Garner, who always said that he treated his slaves as real men. In his mind, Paul D has set schoolteacher's cruel, emasculating, and dehumanizing treatment of him and his fellow slaves in opposition to the more humane treatment of Mr. Garner. Now Paul D begins to follow Halle in questioning whether there really was any essential difference in the slaves' condition under the two men.

Paul D partially blames his despair on his previous belief that he could build a life with Sethe. He believes that he set his goals too high and has consequently suffered a great fall. Yet he locates the beginning of his downfall far in the past, in the tragic outcome of the slaves' escape plan. Halle and Paul A failed to appear at the appointed meeting time, and in their places stood schoolteacher, his nephews, and other white men, waiting for Paul D and Sixo. Sixo's lover, the Thirty-Mile Woman, had escaped, and after he was captured Sixo behaved so maniacally that schoolteacher became convinced he would never again be suitable as a slave. While schoolteacher tried to burn him alive, Sixo only laughed—it was the first time Paul D ever heard him do so. He shouted "Seven-O!" over and over, referring to the baby the Thirty-Mile Woman escaped with inside her.

Schoolteacher and the other men dragged Paul D back home, where he encountered Sethe. Despite the recent disaster, she still intended to run. That was the last time the two saw each other, and Paul D concludes that Sethe's rape and the theft of her milk must have taken place directly afterward. It was in the aftermath of the failed escape that Paul D first learned the price he fetched: nine hundred dollars. The knowledge forever affected his understanding of himself. He wonders what Paul F's price was and what Sethe's would be. He questions whether his life since his aborted escape has been worth it, whether he should have thrown himself into the fire with Sixo.

Chapter 25

Stamp Paid visits Paul D in the church and finds that Paul D has been drinking his troubles away. A white man stops by to ask if the men know Judy of Plank Road. Though Stamp knows her, he feigns ignorance. The white man reprimands Paul D for drinking on church grounds and then rides away. Stamp Paid tells Paul D that during the year that his young master slept with Vashti, Stamp's wife, Stamp Paid did not touch her. When Vashti came to him one night to tell him that she had returned for good, he felt the terrible urge to break her neck. Instead, he says, he changed his name.

The conversation turns to 124, and Stamp Paid tells Paul D that he was present when Sethe tried to kill her children. He defends Sethe's actions, saying she only wanted to "outhurt the hurter." Paul D replies that Sethe scares him but that Beloved scares him more. Stamp Paid asks if Paul D left 124 because of Beloved, but Paul D does not answer.

Analysis

Although Stamp's act of renaming himself signals a kind of spiritual rebirth and reclamation, his new name also testifies to the trauma he has endured under slavery. There is an element of loss in what is otherwise a gesture of strength and self-affirmation. Indeed, in many ways the renaming might be seen as a metaphorical suicide: Stamp had initially wanted to kill one of the masters rather than surrender Vashti, but Vashti had insisted that this would lead only to Stamp's own death and begged him not to undertake the murder. Thus, although Stamp preserved himself out of respect for Vashti's wishes, he denied his natural feelings of rage and assumed a new identity free of emotional ties or bonds. Stamp estranges himself emotionally from Vashti and devotes the rest of his life to helping others pay off "whatever they owed in misery." While Stamp's new identity is assuredly a positive one, it is still born at the expense of the old.

Like Stamp Paid, Paul D is estranged from himself. Since slavery, Paul D has developed emotional coping mechanisms—such as the "tin heart"—that discourage him from loving too passionately and require him to keep his feelings and memories locked away. The novel is full of evidence of Paul D's self-alienation. For example, on one occasion in Georgia, Paul D was unable to tell whether the screaming he heard was coming from himself or from someone else. He often questions his worth, as he does in Chapter 24, and he frequently seems unsure of why he does certain things. For example, he cannot explain why he succumbs to Beloved's seductions, or why he suddenly suggests that he and Sethe have a baby together.

Paul D's thoughts in Chapters 24 and 25 focus on his fear of asserting his humanity, which is something that he had always considered a given before Mr. Garner's death. After Mr. Garner's death and the commencement of schoolteacher's abuses, Paul D learned that his humanity was in fact subject to a white man's whim. A white man could beat it out of him, or even make him want to deny it to himself, as Paul D's contemplation of suicide demonstrates. In retrospect, Paul D doubts whether he was ever truly a man at all, because even Mr. Garner's presumably enlightened version of slavery denied Paul D the power to define his identity as a male and as a thinking, feeling human being. As long as Paul D fears the idea of claiming his humanity, he will continue to feel alienated from himself.

PART THREE: CHAPTER 26

Summary

Like a parasite, Beloved begins to drain Sethe's life force. Sethe arrives at work later and later every morning until she loses her job. The food in the house begins to run low, and Sethe sacrifices her portion for Beloved, who grows fat while Sethe wastes away. Beloved wears Sethe's clothing and copies her mannerisms until Denver has trouble telling them apart. Indeed, their roles merge and invert as Sethe comes to act like a child while Beloved looms over her like a mother. When Sethe tries to assert herself, Beloved reacts violently and breaks things, and the two fight constantly. Sethe points out how much she has suffered for her children, but Beloved accuses her of leaving her behind. Denver begins to fear that Beloved will kill her mother.

Denver decides to leave 124 to find help. Before she can do so, she needs (and gets) some encouragement from the spirit of Baby Suggs, because Denver hasn't left the house by herself in twelve years and fears the outside world. Not knowing where else to turn, Denver goes to the house of her former teacher, Lady Jones.

Although she is part of the black community, Lady Jones has yellow hair and gray eyes. Ironically, Lady Jones was chosen to attend a school in Pennsylvania for "colored" girls because of her light skin. Afterward, she devoted herself to teaching those who were not picked to attend school. Because she loathes her yellow hair, she married the darkest man she could find. She is convinced that everyone, including her own children, despises her and her hair.

Omitting any mention of Beloved, Denver explains that her mother is sick and asks Lady Jones if there is any work she can do in exchange for food. Lady Jones does not know of any work, but she tells everyone at church about Sethe's troubles. Denver begins finding plates and baskets of food on the tree stump in front of 124. Many of them include a slip of paper with the donator's name, and as Denver ventures out to return the containers to their owners she becomes acquainted with the community. Lady Jones also offers her weekly reading lessons.

As the trouble at 124 continues, Denver visits the Bodwins for help. Their black maid, Janey, answers the door and recognizes Denver as a relative of Baby Suggs. Denver tells her about Beloved, and Janey circulates the story around town. Denver secures a job with the Bodwins, but as she leaves their house she is disturbed by the sight of a figurine on display. The statuette is a slave who holds coins in its mouth. At its base is a tag that reads: "At Yo' Service."

Ella hears Denver's story. Although she sees Beloved's tormenting presence as a fair punishment for Sethe's act of infanticide, she does not believe that the punishment is "right," because she believes that past sins should stay in the past. She empathizes with Sethe because she also once refused to care for her child. The child was born of abuse after Ella had been locked up for a year and repeatedly raped by a father and son. Ella decides to rally a group of roughly thirty black women to exorcise Beloved from 124. They march to Sethe's house, where Denver is waiting for Mr. Bodwin to pick her up for work.

When Sethe and Beloved hear the women begin to sing, they go outside to the porch. The women see Sethe, small and shrunken, standing next to a beautiful, naked, pregnant woman. Sethe spots Mr. Bodwin coming up the road and mistakes him for schoolteacher. She rushes from the porch waving an ice pick, leaving Beloved alone. Beloved watches as Denver also leaves her side to chase after Sethe. All the women rush to prevent Sethe from killing Mr. Bodwin. At the beginning of the next chapter, we will learn what happened next through the narration of Stamp Paid: apparently, Ella punched Sethe before she could attack Mr. Bodwin, and the women held her down; then, after subduing Sethe, the women looked up to find that Beloved had disappeared.

Analysis

As Sethe's only remaining child, Denver represents the future. In Part Three, Denver transforms from a girl into a woman and begins, for the first time, to develop an independent sense of self. She serves as a bridge between Sethe and the rest of the community, and she provides Sethe with an opportunity to escape the haunting memories and sins of the past. She feels a sense of responsibility for her mother, who grows weaker and weaker in the shadows of Beloved's power and of her own guilt. Ironically, Sethe's regression toward infancy triggers Denver's maturation.

While Denver represents the future, Beloved, of course, represents the past. Throughout the book, Beloved stands for the haunting legacy of slavery. As her presence becomes a danger to the whole black community, we see that the consequences of slavery haunt not only individuals but whole networks of people. Correspondingly, Beloved's exorcism will provide a catharsis for the town's entire black population as well as for Sethe. It is significant that it will take the community as a whole to rid 124 of Beloved—to exorcise the universal ghostly presence of slavery.

At the same time, it takes one woman, with her own personal sense of past suffering, to organize and lead the exorcism. Due to her own painful relationship with the past, Ella is the most attuned to the invasive and harmful aspect of Beloved's resurrection. When Ella decides to rid the community of Beloved's presence, she leads an exorcism of past traumas as well as of past sins. She wipes away the legacies of slavery's evils and the memories of the evils that slavery induced in its victims, such as Ella's own rejection of her baby.

Sethe's mistaking of Mr. Bodwin for schoolteacher during the exorcism indicates the extent to which she is immersed in the past. Instead of simply repeating the past by running to protect her own children, Sethe does what she wishes she had done before: she attacks the perceived enemy. Schoolteacher is not really present, though, and Sethe's violence is certainly misdirected. She nearly kills Mr. Bodwin, who not only helped Baby Suggs but also fought for Sethe's release from jail and is now trying to help her daughter find work. Thus, while Sethe does reenact her past mistake in a way, this time the mistake will not prove tragic; instead, it opens the door to potential growth. Just as this episode gives Sethe the chance to revise and emend the actions that have haunted her for eighteen years, it also grants the townswomen the opportunity to revisit and adjust their own past behavior. One of the reasons schoolteacher's visit years ago ended so tragically was that the community had failed to warn Sethe of his approach. Now, the townswomen take decisive action to stop Sethe from doing something she will regret later. The individual and the community work together to learn from past mistakes and to heal themselves.

In many ways, *Beloved* itself functions as a kind of exorcism. Morrison creates a space for both the victims and the perpetrators of oppression to confront and narrate their pasts. As readers and as heirs to American and world history, we are able to gain understanding of, and thus control over, prior sorrows and crimes. Through the confrontation of a dehumanizing past, humanity can be affirmed. Morrison suggests that we must learn to confront the past both as individuals *and* as a community before we can truly begin to extinguish its dangerous legacies.

PART THREE: CHAPTERS 27–28

Summary

Chapter 27

Stamp Paid tells Paul D about the recent events at 124. The old man says that he no longer hears the voices around the house that he used to and that Beloved disappeared in the chaos that followed Sethe's attempted attack on Mr. Bodwin. A small boy said he saw a naked woman running through the woods with fish for hair, but no one has seen her since.

Paul D asks Denver if she believes Beloved really was her baby sister who had come back from the other side. Denver replies that she believes Beloved to have been her sister, but, at times, she thinks Beloved was more. Denver continues to work for Miss Bodwin, who is giving her informal academic training in the hopes of sending Denver to Oberlin College. Denver warns Paul D to speak kindly to Sethe, who has not yet recovered entirely. Paul D walks to 124 and thinks about the series of escapes he has undertaken in his life. He ran from Sweet Home; he ran from Alfred, Georgia; and, during the war, he worked for both sides and ran from both. After the war, he thought he was free to walk the roads, but he saw dead blacks strewn everywhere, including women and children—he still had to keep running. Paul D wonders why he ran from Sethe.

When Paul D reaches 124, he senses that Beloved has left forever. He finds Sethe lying in Baby Suggs's bed with vacant eyes. He fears that, like Baby Suggs before her, Sethe wants simply to lie down and wait for death. He tells her that he wants to help Denver take care of her. She replies miserably that her "best thing" has left her again, and Paul D wonders at the range of emotions that Sethe inspires in him. Sixo once told him that his Thirty-Mile Woman inspired his love because she gathered up the jumbled pieces of him and gave them back to him in order. Paul thinks that Sethe does the same for him. She helps him to stop being ashamed of his past, and he notes that when he is with her, the memories of being collared and muzzled like a beast no longer have the power to steal his manhood from him. He tells her they have more of "yesterday" than they need and that they need more "tomorrow" to make the "yesterday" bearable. Taking her hand, he tells Sethe that she shouldn't consider Beloved's departure to be the departure of her "best thing." Sethe, and not her children, is her "own best thing."

Chapter 28

As though Beloved were a bad dream, everyone tries to forget her. The community sees her as the representative of an implacable loneliness that cannot be soothed or rocked away. Never satisfied, it roams and devours. Sethe, Denver, and Paul D take longer to forget Beloved than the townspeople do. Nevertheless, after a while they realize they cannot remember or repeat a single thing she said. In fact, they cannot say with certainty that she was ever really there.

Analysis

When Paul D first showed up at the doorstep of 124, he seemed aware of the necessity of confronting the past in order to escape its grip. He assured Sethe that with him there to pull her out, she should feel safe about venturing "inside" her painful memories. When Beloved's arrival forces Sethe to face the past, these memories begin, as Sethe feared, to consume her completely. Only with the help of those around her can Sethe escape Beloved's hold. Denver keeps Sethe alive, the community helps to expel Beloved, and Paul D supports Sethe by telling her that she, and not her children, is her own "best thing." By dealing with the past, Sethe and Paul D secure the possibility of enjoying a future together.

As a novel, *Beloved* performs a similar function. The book catalogs a past that contemporary readers must contend with before moving forward. Throughout most of the book, the omniscient narrator filters almost all of the story through the various perspectives of Sethe, Paul D, Denver, Baby Suggs, Stamp Paid, schoolteacher, Lady Jones, Mr. Bodwin, Beloved, and Ella. However, in the short, closing chapter of the book, Morrison diverges from this strategy and returns the narration to a more universalized, abstracted, and distanced voice. The result is poetic: words rhyme and phrases repeat, affecting an almost trancelike state in the reader. Morrison punctuates these mesmerizing, cadenced paragraphs, which describe how everyone gradually forgot Beloved, with the blunt explanation, "It was not a story to pass on." Enigmatically, this phrase evolves, by the chapter's end, into a warning: "This is not a story to pass on." And yet, of course, *Beloved* does pass that story on. Its very purpose is to restore a history to a people whose history has been erased by centuries of willed forgetfulness and forced silence. Perhaps the narrator's warning is intended to remind us that it is not easy to keep that history in our memory. Nor is it necessarily helpful for us to remember that history if it is not conveyed with responsibility and sensitivity. Resurrecting the past is a painful process, and, in some ways, *Beloved* is an emotionally painful book to read. Like its title character, it is a difficult entity to contend with, one that can inspire or distress the reader with equal intensity. Yet, by engaging with this disturbing, unrelenting force in a conscientious way, we may begin to understand the past, as well as its impact on our present.

IMPORTANT QUOTATIONS EXPLAINED

1. 124 was spiteful. Full of a baby's venom.

Each of *Beloved*'s three parts begins with an observation about 124, the house occupied by Sethe and her daughter Denver. Part One of the novel begins with this quotation, Part Two with "124 was loud," and Part Three with "124 was quiet." 124 is haunted by the abusive and malevolent spirit of Sethe's dead daughter. When the novel opens, the ghost rages with a fury that is most definitely a baby's. In Chapter 5, however, the baby ghost manifests herself in the form of Beloved, who seems to be a reincarnation of the baby Sethe murdered eighteen years ago. As the novel progresses, Beloved will become more powerful, until, in Chapter 19, she is said to wield the force of a collective "black and angry dead." The spirit will wreak havoc on 124 until the community exorcises Beloved in Chapter 26.

2. Whitepeople believed that whatever the manners, under every dark skin was a jungle. Swift unnavigable waters, swinging screaming baboons, sleeping snakes, red gums ready for their sweet white blood. In a way . . . they were right. . . . But it wasn't the jungle blacks brought with them to this place. . . . It was the jungle whitefolks planted in them. And it grew. It spread . . . until it invaded the whites who had made it. . . . Made them bloody, silly, worse than even they wanted to be, so scared were they of the jungle they had made. The screaming baboon lived under their own white skin; the red gums were their own.

In Chapter 19, at the beginning of Part Two, Stamp Paid considers the ways in which slavery corrupts and dehumanizes everyone who comes in contact with it, including the white slave owners. It makes them fearful, sadistic, and raving. For example, one could say that schoolteacher's perverse lessons and violent racism exist because they are his means of justifying the institution of slavery. In his thoughts, Stamp Paid depicts the jungle from a white person's point of view—as awesome, exotic, and thrilling. He perceives anxiety on the part of the whites about the unknown, unintelligible, "unnavigable" psyche of the slaves they steal. The sense of anxiety is emphasized by the images of wild consumption in the passage—jungles growing and spreading, red gums ready for blood. The conclusion of this passage asserts that what the whites recognize and run from is in fact their own savagery. They project this savagery onto those whom they perceive to be their opposites—"the Other." The passage derives its power from the way Morrison moves the images of the jungle around, so that, by the end, the whites are the ones who hide a jungle under their skin; they are consuming themselves.

3. Saying more might push them both to a place they couldn't get back from. He would keep the rest where it belonged: in that tobacco tin buried in his chest where a red heart used to be. Its lid rusted shut.

In Chapter 7, Paul D begins sharing his painful memories with Sethe, but he fears that revealing too much will wrench the two former slaves back into a past from which they might never escape. Both Sethe and Paul D avoid the pain of their past as best they can, and both have developed elaborate and ultimately destructive coping mechanisms to keep the past at bay. Sethe has effectively erased much of her memory, and Paul D functions by locking his memories and emotions away in his imagined "tobacco tin." The rustiness of the tin contributes to the reader's sense of the inaccessibility and corrosiveness of Paul D's memories. His separation from his emotions means he is alienated from himself, but Paul D is willing to pay the price to keep himself from his painful and turbulent past. When Paul D is forced to confront the past during his erotic encounter with Beloved, the rusted lid of his heart begins to break open. At the end of the novel, Paul D reveals that he is willing finally to risk emotional safety and open himself to another person, to love Sethe.

4. . . . [I]f you go there—you who was never there—if you go there and stand in the place where it was, it will happen again; it will be there, waiting for you . . . [E]ven though it's all over—over and done with—it's going to always be there waiting for you.

This passage is from Chapter 3. In her "emerald closet," Denver remembers what Sethe once told about the indestructible nature of the past. According to Sethe's theory of time, past traumas continue to reenact themselves indefinitely, so it is possible to stumble into someone else's unhappy memory. Accordingly, although Sethe describes for Denver what "was," she turns to the future tense and tells her that the past will "always be there waiting for you." Sethe pictures the past as a physical presence, something that is "there," that fills a space. Beloved's arrival confirms this notion of history's corporeality.

The force of the past is evident even in the difficulty Sethe has speaking about it. She stutters, backtracks, and repeats herself as though mere words cannot do justice to her subject matter. Even in this passage, as she warns Denver against the inescapability of the past, Sethe enacts and illustrates the very phenomenon she describes. She repeats her warning several times in a manner that demonstrates the recurrence of ideas and her inability to leave past thoughts behind. Sethe's warnings are the main cause of Denver's fears of leaving 124 and of the community. Only in Chapter 26 does Denver finally venture out alone. She realizes that even if she succeeds in preventing chance encounters with the past, the past may nevertheless actively begin to come after her.

5. And if she thought anything, it was No. No. Nono. Nonono. Simple. She just flew. Collected every bit of life she had made, all the parts of her that were precious and fine and beautiful, and carried, pushed, dragged them through the veil, out, away, over there where no one could hurt them. Over there. Outside this place, where they would be safe.

After Paul D learns about Sethe's crime from Stamp Paid in Chapter 18, he goes to 124 in search of an explanation. This passage, although written in the third person, records Sethe's thoughts. Sethe saw the decision she made as "simple." She wanted to secure her children's safety, to send them "over there" into the afterlife rather than let them be pulled back to Sweet Home with schoolteacher. Sethe's passion for her children, which infuses so much of the novel, shines through in this passage with particular clarity. The moment Sethe's reason reduced itself to instinct, her language broke down as well: she recalls her words as "No. No. Nono. Nonono." For her, the border between life and death is tenuous, nothing more than a screen or "veil" that she hopes to place in front of her children.

Another significant aspect of the passage is Sethe's identification of her children as "the parts of her that were precious and fine and beautiful"; for Sethe, to allow schoolteacher to take her children would be to allow him to destroy everything that is good in herself, to destroy all the "life" she had made. According to this understanding, Sethe's murder of her daughter seems a less legally and morally reprehensible crime because it becomes an act of self-defense. Yet the question of Sethe's guilt is never fully settled in the book. The characters debate the morality of her act in pointed language, but Morrison herself withholds judgment on the deed. Throughout the book, she focuses her criticisms instead on the forces of slavery that led Sethe to kill her own daughter. In this passage and elsewhere, Morrison condemns slavery as an institution so perverse that it could mutate a mother's love into murder.

KEY FACTS

FULL TITLE
Beloved

AUTHOR
Toni Morrison

TYPE OF WORK
Novel

GENRE
Historical fiction; ghost story

LANGUAGE
English

TIME AND PLACE WRITTEN
The 1980s in Albany, New York

DATE OF FIRST PUBLICATION
1987

PUBLISHER
Alfred A. Knopf, Inc.

NARRATOR
Beloved's primary narrator is anonymous and omniscient. However, in parts of the book the narration is taken over by the characters themselves. Chapters 20 through 23, for example, consist of three monologues and a chorus. At other points in the book, the characters act as visiting narrators of a sort, who relate and comment on events.

POINT OF VIEW
The anonymous narrator of *Beloved* speaks in the third person and withholds judgment on the actions described. When the characters serve as narrators, they generally use the first person and openly express their personal opinions.

TONE

The text's tone changes from character to character and reflects their varying, usually explicit attitudes toward the events. The primary "narrator," however, seems to regard the characters and their actions with a mixture of mournfulness, regret, and awe.

TENSE

Beloved fluctuates in tense between the immediate and distant pasts. It also includes occasional, jarring transitions to the present tense.

SETTING (TIME)

1873, with frequent flashbacks to the early 1850s

SETTING (PLACE)

Cincinnati, Ohio; flashbacks to Sweet Home plantation in Kentucky and prison in Alfred, Georgia

PROTAGONIST

Sethe is the primary protagonist, but Denver also drives much of the plot's action, especially in Part Three.

MAJOR CONFLICT

Having survived a traumatic escape from slavery, Sethe has killed her older daughter in a mad attempt to keep her from being taken back to the South by her old master. A mysterious figure now appears at Sethe's home, calling herself by the name on the dead daughter's tombstone.

RISING ACTION

A ghost has haunted Sethe and Denver's house for several years. Paul D arrives and chases the ghost away. Beloved appears at the house soon after and causes memories to surface in Sethe, Denver, and Paul D.

CLIMAX

Because the novel follows two different stories, one told through flashbacks and one that is taking place in the novel's present, there are two different climaxes. The climax of the flashback plot occurs near the end of Part One in Chapter 16, when the text finally reveals the circumstances of Sethe's daughter's death: eighteen years ago, Sethe attempted to murder all her children when she refused to hand them over to schoolteacher to endure a life of slavery. Only her elder daughter died. The second climax occurs at the end of the novel, during the "exorcism" of Beloved, who seems to be the ghost of the daughter Sethe murdered. In an echo of the first climax, Sethe mistakes Mr. Bodwin, her family's benefactor, for schoolteacher and tries to kill him with an ice pick.

FALLING ACTION

Beloved leaves 124 forever, Denver is preparing to go to college, and Paul D returns to Sethe, who has been spending her days in Baby Suggs's bed.

THEMES

Slavery's destruction of identity; the importance of community solidarity; the powers and limits of language

MOTIFS

The supernatural; allusions to Christianity

SYMBOLS

The color red; trees; the tin tobacco box

FORESHADOWING

Morrison unfolds the story in a circular, elusive way, making use of a device akin to, but more complex than, foreshadowing. The narrative makes indirect or incomplete allusions to events that are picked up and developed further at later points in the novel. For example, the death of Sethe's daughter is mentioned repeatedly from the beginning of the novel, but only in Chapter 18 does the complete story unfold.

STUDY QUESTIONS AND ESSAY TOPICS

Study Questions

1. *How does Beloved function as an alter ego for Sethe?*

In *Beloved,* Sethe persistently conflates her identity with that of her child. Sethe inadvertently named Beloved after herself. When the minister at her daughter's funeral addressed the living (including Sethe) as "Dearly Beloved," she believed he was referring to her dead daughter. Rather than engraving her child's real name on her tombstone, she engraved "Beloved," a name that now refers both to herself and to the baby. Sethe feels debased and dehumanized by her experiences as a slave and thus cannot love herself. Instead, she puts all the energy that should be spent on loving herself into loving her children. Her own identity is defined entirely in terms of motherhood. Sethe herself cannot conceive of the word "beloved" as referring to herself but only to her child; she regards her children as the "best part" of herself. Because Beloved's name refers to Sethe as well, and because Sethe defines her children as part of herself, Beloved functions as a sort of alter ego for Sethe.

Beloved also functions on a more general level as Sethe's repressed memories, as her personal past. As such, she is another sort of alter ego. Beloved is the self that Sethe has tried to forget, to discard. When Sethe finally learns to confront her memories, she rejoins and comes to terms with her past self.

2. *One could say that the community judges Sethe harshly out of a desire to displace its own guilt. What evidence would support such a conclusion?*

The specific comments made by Sethe's critics help us to identify the underlying motivations of their harsh condemnations. Ella, for example, accuses Sethe of excessive pride and labels Sethe's act of infanticide unjustified. However, Ella herself committed infanticide, though in a more indirect manner: when she gave birth to a child who was the result of repeated rape by a white man and his son, Ella refused to care for it because she considered such forced motherhood to be demeaning, and the baby died. It seems that Ella's condemnation of Sethe allows her to avoid confronting her own feelings of guilt. Similarly, Paul D tells Sethe that she acted like an "animal" when she killed her children. Yet we know that Paul D's most profound insecurity lies in his fear that he is less than a man: he is haunted by the dehumanizing experiences of slavery, during which he realized that Sweet Home's rooster was allowed more manhood than he, and during which he was forced to wear an iron bit like a horse.

From these examples we can infer that the general community's criticism of Sethe may stem from the same sort of guilt. The townspeople certainly have reason to feel guilty: their jealousy of Baby Suggs's celebratory feast led them to fail to warn Sethe or Baby Suggs that schoolteacher had arrived to hunt down Sethe and her children. Judging Sethe for killing her child allows them to avoid acknowledging the role they played in the creation of the circumstances that drove Sethe to murder.

3. *How can Sethe and Paul D be seen as perpetual fugitives?*

Paul D spends years wandering from one place to another. After his horrifying experiences with schoolteacher and prison, he refuses to love anything strongly. In order to avoid establishing long-term relationships, he wanders from place to place. In symbolic terms, Paul D rejects his "red heart" and replaces it with a tightly sealed "tin tobacco box." In protecting himself from further heartache, Paul D remains a fugitive from his own humanity.

At the beginning of the novel, Sethe says that she will not leave 124 because she will never run from another thing in her life. Nevertheless, she is always fleeing her own memories. Instead of confronting her past, Sethe vigilantly tries to keep always ahead of it, always above it. By turning and engaging with her past, which Beloved's appearance enables her to do, Sethe is able finally to preempt and lessen its blows.

Suggested Essay Topics

1. How does Beloved help Denver gain an independent identity? How might the dynamic between Beloved and Denver represent the effect of history on subsequent generations?

2. Both Stamp Paid and Baby Suggs have given themselves their own names: what is the significance of this? What does the act of renaming signify? What does it say about the characters who engage in it?

3. The novel is packed with supernatural events. For example, Baby Suggs has premonitions, Stamp Paid hears voices, and Beloved seems to be some sort of ghost. How do supernatural phenomena refute schoolteacher's "scientific" approach to the world? The text suggests more than once that Beloved may be an ordinary woman recently escaped from years of captivity. Why might the book make this move to "explain" the supernatural? Significantly, Lady Jones, another, though kindly, "schoolteacher" also refutes supernatural explanations. She is skeptical of Denver's story about Beloved and considers the town ignorant for believing it. What effect does this have on the reader's own interpretation of the seemingly magical events in *Beloved*?

4. The novel is narrated from the perspectives of former slaves and their families. At different points we get Sethe's, Paul D's, Stamp Paid's, Baby Suggs's, Beloved's, Lady Jones's, and Ella's varying points of view. Yet the climax of the novel—Sethe's act of infanticide—is depicted according to schoolteacher's point of view. Why does Morrison choose to disclose the circumstances of Sethe's tragedy as they appeared to schoolteacher? How does this influence the reader's reaction to the story?

REVIEW AND RESOURCES

QUIZ

1. Where is 124 located?

A. Alfred, Georgia
B. Baton Rouge, Louisiana
C. Just outside of Cincinnati, Ohio
D. Wilmington, Delaware

2. Who tells Sethe that her scars resemble a chokecherry tree?

A. Amy Denver
B. Paul D
C. Baby Suggs
D. Beloved

3. What does Sethe do while under the delusion that Mr. Bodwin is schoolteacher, who has come to take her back to Sweet Home?

A. She flees 124 with Denver and Beloved
B. She commits suicide
C. She orders him to leave her home
D. She tries to kill him with an ice pick

4. Where does Denver habitually go to find solitude and solace?

A. A grove she calls her emerald closet
B. The Clearing
C. Church
D. Lady Jones's house

5. Which set of schoolteacher's lessons does Sethe find most shocking?

A. His lessons on lynching
B. His lessons on forgiveness, generosity, and Christian love
C. His lessons on her animal characteristics
D. His lessons on sexual violation

6. *What is Beloved doing when Sethe first sees her?*
   A. Swimming in a stream
   B. Sleeping near the steps of 124
   C. Walking home from the carnival with Denver
   D. Trembling in the woodshed

7. *What allows Paul D to escape from prison in Georgia?*
   A. A prison uprising
   B. A feigned illness
   C. Mr. Garner's intervention
   D. A rainstorm

8. *What is signaled by the return of Here Boy?*
   A. Beloved's departure
   B. The failure of Reconstruction
   C. Halle's death
   D. Baby Suggs's presence

9. *What prevents Baby Suggs from sensing schoolteacher's approach?*
   A. A sudden loss of hearing and sight
   B. Fatigue from the previous night's party
   C. Lack of cooperation from the black community
   D. Her rejection of religion

10. *Who saves Denver's life in the woodshed?*
   A. Stamp Paid
   B. Beloved
   C. The Thirty-Mile Woman
   D. Howard and Buglar

11. *Why does Denver stop going to Lady Jones's school?*
   A. She can't afford to pay the tuition
   B. A fellow student asks about her mother's past
   C. She feels disturbed by Lady Jones's self-loathing
   D. Sethe wants her to stay at home

12. Who helps Sethe find safety after she escapes from Sweet Home?
A. Paul D, Paul F, and Paul A
B. Paul D, Stamp Paid, and Halle
C. Amy, Janey, and Lady Jones
D. Amy, Stamp Paid, and Ella

13. Where is Denver born?
A. In Baby Suggs's bedroom
B. In a cornfield at Sweet Home
C. In a boat
D. In a hospital in Cincinnati

14. Where does Miss Bodwin want to send Denver?
A. To a job in a shirt factory
B. To Oberlin College
C. To a school for black girls in Pennsylvania
D. To Paris

15. Who are the "men without skin"?
A. White men that haunt Beloved's thoughts
B. Sethe's dead ancestors
C. Male slaves who have lost claim over their manhood
D. Traumatized ex-slaves who have numbed themselves to all pain

16. According to Paul D and Sethe, why does Halle slather butter on his face?
A. Schoolteacher forces him to do it as part of an "experiment"
B. He wants to soothe his skin after imagining Sixo's burning
C. He wants to convince Mrs. Garner he is insane so she will free him
D. Watching schoolteacher's nephews violate Sethe makes him go mad

17. After whom is Denver named?
A. The young white girl who delivers her
B. The city of Sethe's birth
C. A kind of wildflower
D. The Denver River

18. *By whom does Denver believe Sethe is being choked as they sit in the Clearing?*
   A. Baby Suggs's ghost
   B. The malevolent energy of the community
   C. Schoolteacher
   D. Beloved

19. *What causes Denver to lose her hearing temporarily?*
   A. She hears the story of her father's madness
   B. Her ears are damaged by excessively loud music at the carnival
   C. She asks Sethe whether she was put in jail for murder but goes deaf before she can listen to the answer
   D. She hears her sister's screams as Sethe murders her

20. *How does Denver regain her hearing?*
   A. Baby Suggs blesses her
   B. She hears the dead baby's ghost crawling upstairs
   C. Beloved tells her about the afterlife
   D. Sethe bathes her head in the stream

21. *What finally convinces Sethe that Beloved is her daughter's ghost?*
   A. Beloved asks where Sethe's earrings are
   B. Beloved's breath smells of milk
   C. Sethe sees the scar under Beloved's chin
   D. Beloved hums a song that Sethe made up to sing to her children

22. *What disconcerts Denver as she leaves the Bodwins' house?*
   A. A figurine of a black slave
   B. Mr. Bodwin's use of racial slurs
   C. A collection of books about the inferiority of the black race
   D. The sudden apparition of Baby Suggs's ghost

23. *What sudden memory concerning her mother most shocks Sethe?*
   A. Her mother had a mark burned into her skin in the shape of a circle and cross
   B. Her mother was hanged when Sethe was a child
   C. Her mother killed all of her other babies
   D. Her mother spoke a language Sethe no longer remembers

24. *When does Paul D tell Sethe she is her own "best thing"?*
   A. When he asks her to have a child with him
   B. When he returns to her at the end of the novel
   C. When they walk home from the carnival
   D. After he tells her about the last time he saw Halle

25. *How does Denver regard her father?*
   A. As a selfish man who abandoned his family
   B. As a brave man who was shot by schoolteacher
   C. As a cowardly man who watched his wife being raped but failed to intervene
   D. As an angelic man who will return one day

Answer Key:
1: C; 2: A; 3: D; 4: A; 5: C; 6: B; 7: D; 8: A; 9: C; 10: A; 11: B; 12: D; 13: C; 14: B; 15: A; 16: D; 17: A; 18: D; 19: C; 20: B; 21: D; 22: A; 23: C; 24: B; 25: D

SUGGESTIONS FOR FURTHER READING

Carmean, Karen. *Toni Morrison's World of Fiction.* Troy, NY: Whitson Publishing Company, 1993.

Conner, Marc C., ed. *The Aesthetics of Toni Morrison: Speaking the Unspeakable.* Jackson: University Press of Mississippi, 2000.

David, Ron. *Toni Morrison Explained: A Reader's Road Map to the Novels.* New York: Random House, 2000.

Grewal, Gurleen. *Circles of Sorrow, Lines of Struggle: The Novels of Toni Morrison.* Baton Rouge: Louisiana State University Press, 1998.

Holden-Kirwan, Jennifer L. "Looking into the Self That Is No Self: An Examination of Subjectivity in *Beloved,*" *African American Review* 32, no. 3 (1998): 415–26.

Middleton, David L., ed. *Toni Morrison's Fiction: Contemporary Criticism.* New York: Garland Publishing, 1997.

Page, Philip. *Dangerous Freedom: Fusion and Fragmentation in Toni Morrison's Novels.* Jackson: University Press of Mississippi, 1995.

Solomon, Barbara H., ed. *Critical Essays on Toni Morrison's* Beloved. New York: G. K. Hall, 1998.

Sumana, K. *The Novels of Toni Morrison: A Study in Race, Gender and Class.* New Delhi: Prestige Books, 1998.

THE SPARKNOTES LITERATURE LIBRARY

1984
Absalom, Absalom!
The Adventures of Tom Sawyer
The Aeneid
Agamemnon
Alice in Wonderland and Through the Looking Glass
All Quiet on the Western Front
All the King's Men
All the Pretty Horses
And Then There Were None
Animal Farm
Anna Karenina
As I Lay Dying
Atlas Shrugged
The Autobiography of Benjamin Franklin
The Awakening
Babbitt
The Bell Jar
Beloved
Beowulf
Billy Budd
Black Boy
Bless Me, Ultima
The Bluest Eye
Brave New World
The Call of the Wild
Candide
Cannery Row
The Canterbury Tales
Cat's Cradle
Catch-22
The Catcher in the Rye
The Chosen
A Christmas Carol
A Clockwork Orange
The Color Purple
A Connecticut Yankee in King Arthur's Court
Crime and Punishment
The Crucible
Cry, the Beloved Country
The Crying of Lot 49
Cyrano de Bergerac
Daisy Miller
David Copperfield
Death in Venice
Death of a Salesman
The Diary of Anne Frank
Doctor Faustus
A Doll's House
Don Quixote
Dr. Jekyll and Mr. Hyde
Dr. Zhivago
Dracula
Dubliners
Emma
An Enemy of the People
Ethan Frome
Fahrenheit 451
Fallen Angels
Far from the Madding Crowd
A Farewell to Arms
Farewell to Manzanar
The Fellowship of the Ring
For Whom the Bell Tolls
The Fountainhead
Frankenstein
Franny and Zooey
Ghosts
Gilgamesh
The Giver
The Glass Menagerie
Go Down, Moses
Go Tell it on the Mountain
The Good Earth
The Grapes of Wrath
Great Expectations
The Great Gatsby
Grendel
Gulliver's Travels
The Handmaid's Tale
Hard Times
Heart of Darkness
Hedda Gabler
The Hobbit
The House of Mirth
The House on Mango Street
Howards End
Huckleberry Finn
I Know Why the Caged Bird Sings
I Never Promised You a Rose Garden
The Iliad
The Importance of Being Earnest
In Cold Blood
In Our Time
Inherit the Wind
Invisible Man
Ivanhoe
Jane Eyre
Johnny Tremain
The Joy Luck Club
Jude the Obscure
The Jungle
Lady Chatterley's Lover
The Last of the Mohicans
Les Misérables
Light in August
Like Water for Chocolate
The Little Prince
Little Women

Lolita
Long Day's Journey into Night
Looking Backward
Lord Jim
Lord of the Flies
Madame Bovary
Maggie: A Girl of the Streets
Mansfield Park
The Martian Chronicles
The Mayor of Casterbridge
Medea
The Metamorphosis
Middlemarch
Moby Dick
A Modest Proposal
Moll Flanders
Mrs. Dalloway
My Antonia
Narrative of the Life of Frederick Douglass
Native Son
Nausea
The New Testament
Night
No Exit
Notes from Underground
O Pioneers!
The Odyssey
The Oedipus Trilogy
Of Mice and Men
The Old Man and the Sea
Oliver Twist
On the Road
The Once and Future King
One Day in the Life of Ivan Denisovich
One Flew Over the Cuckoo's Nest
One Hundred Years of Solitude
Ordinary People
Our Town
The Outsiders
A Passage to India
The Pearl
The Picture of Dorian Gray
The Plague
Poe's Short Stories
A Portrait of the Artist as a Young Man
A Prayer for Owen Meany
Pride and Prejudice
Pudd'nhead Wilson
Pygmalion
A Raisin in the Sun
Rebecca
The Red Badge of Courage
The Red Pony
The Red and the Black
The Return of the Native
Robinson Crusoe
Roll of Thunder, Hear My Cry
A Room of One's Own
A Room with a View
The Scarlet Letter
Sense and Sensibility
A Separate Peace
Siddhartha
Silas Marner
Sir Gawain and the Green Knight
Sister Carrie
Slaughterhouse-Five
Snow Falling on Cedars
Song of Roland
Song of Solomon
Sons and Lovers
The Sound and the Fury
Steppenwolf
The Stranger
A Streetcar Named Desire
Sula
The Sun Also Rises
Swann's Way
A Tale of Two Cities
Tender is the Night
Tess of the d'Urbervilles
Their Eyes Were Watching God
Things Fall Apart
This Side of Paradise
The Three Musketeers
The Time Machine
To Kill a Mockingbird
To the Lighthouse
Treasure Island
The Trial
Tristram Shandy
The Turn of the Screw
Uncle Tom's Cabin
Waiting for Godot
Walden
Where the Red Fern Grows
White Fang
Who's Afraid of Virginia Woolf?
Winesburg, Ohio
A Wrinkle in Time
Wuthering Heights

SPARKNOTES BEYOND LITERATURE: ACCESS THE ENTIRE COLLECTION AT WWW.SPARKNOTES.COM

ASTRONOMY
Earth
Jupiter
Mars
Mercury
Neptune
Pluto
Saturn
The Sun
Uranus
Venus

BIOGRAPHY
Abraham Lincoln
Albert Einstein
Galileo Galilei
Isaac Newton
Joan of Arc
John F. Kennedy
Joseph Stalin
Leonardo da Vinci
Martin Luther King, Jr.
Mohandas Gandhi
Napoleon Bonaparte
Pablo Picasso
Queen Elizabeth I
Sacajawea
Thomas Jefferson
Vladimir Lenin

BIOLOGY
Animal Behavior
Behavioral Ecology
The Cell Cycle
Cell Differences
Cell Membranes
Cell Reproduction
Cell Respiration
Cell Structure
The Citric Acid Cycle
DNA Replication and Repair
DNA Transcription
Darwin
Evolution
Fungi
Genetics
Glycolysis
Instinct
Intracellular Components
Lamarck
Life Cycle
Macroevolution
Meiosis
Microorganisms
Mitosis
Modern Synthesis
Molecular Biology
Monera
Natural Selection
Orientation and Navigation
Plant Classification
Plant Structures
Population Genetics
RNA Processing
Protista
Reproduction Isolation
Signaling and Communication
Speciation
Structure of Nucleic Acids
Translation
Viruses

CHEMISTRY
Acids and Bases
Atomic Structure
Bonding
Buffers
Carbocycles
Chemistry
Colligative Properties
Conformations
Covalent Bonds
Electrochemistry
Electrolytic Cells
Enantiomers and Diastereomers
Galvanic Cells
Ideal Gases
Ionic Bonds
Kinetic Molecular Theory
Molecular Orbitals
Orbitals
Organic Chemistry
The Periodic Table
Pressure
Rate Laws
Reaction Kinetics
Reaction Mechanisms
Real Gases
Real World Reactions
Sn1E1 Reactions
Sn2E2 Reactions
Solubility
Stereochemistry
Stereoisomers
Stoichiometry
Structure of Alkanes
Thermodynamics
Titrations
Units, Scientific Notation, and Significant Figures
pH Calculations

ECONOMICS
Banking
Economic Growth
Elasticity
Equilibrium
Income Distribution
International Trade
Labor Markets
Macroeconomics
Measuring the Economy
Microeconomics
Monopolies & Oligopolies
Policy Debates
Supply and Demand
Tax and Fiscal Policy

HISTORY
American Revolution
The Articles of Confederation
Building the State
The Civil Rights Movement
Civil War
The Declaration of Independence
Early Middle Ages
The Enlightenment
Europe: 1815-1848
Europe: 1848-1871
Europe: 1871-1914
The Fall of Rome
The Federalist Papers
The First Years of the Union
The French Revolution
The French and Indian War
The Gilded Age
The Great Depression
High Middle Ages
The Interwar Years
Italian Renaissance
The Korean War
Napoleonic Europe
Pre-Civil War
The Revolutionary War
The Roman Empire
The Russian Revolution
The Scientific Revolution
The Spanish-American War
The United States Constitution
The Vietnam War
The War of 1812
Westward Expansion
World War I
World War II

MATHEMATICS
3-D Measurements
Absolute Value
Algebra I
Algebra II
Angles
Axioms and Postulates
Binomial Expansion
Brain Teasers
Building Blocks
Calculus AB
Calculus BC I
Calculus BC II
Circles
Complex Numbers
Compound Inequalities
Computing Derivatives
Computing Integrals
Congruence
Conic Sections
Constructions
Continuity and Limits
Decimals
Definite Integral
The Derivative
Discrete Functions
Exponential Functions
Exponential and Logarithmic Functions
Exponents
Expressions and Equations
Factoring
Fractions
Functions
Functions, Limits, and Continuity
Geometric Proofs
Geometric Surfaces
Geometry I
Geometry II

Geometry III
Graphing Data
Graphing Equations
Inductive and Deductive Reasoning
Inequalities
Integers and Rationals
Introduction to Derivatives
Introduction to Integrals
Inverse, Exponential, and Logarithmic Functions
Logarithmic Functions
Logic Statements
Matrices
Measurements
Operations
Parametric Equations
Parametric and Polar Curves
Percents
Perimeter and Area
Polygons
Polynomial Functions
Polynomials
Powers, Exponents, and Roots
Prealgebra
Precalculus
Probability
Quadratics
Rational Expressions
Sequences and Series
Solving Oblique Triangles
Solving Right Triangles
Special Graphs
Special Triangles
Systems of Equations
Systems of Three Equations
The Taylor Series
Theorems
Trigonometry
Variables
Variation
Whole Numbers

NUTRITION

Addiction
Amino Acids and Proteins
Carbohydrates
Lipids and Coronary Heart Disease
Major Minerals
Minerals
Minor Minerals
Nutritional Assessment and Profiling
Sexually Transmitted Diseases
Vitamins

PHILOSOPHY

The Apology
Beyond Good and Evil
Civil Disobedience
The Communist Manifesto
Confessions
Crito
An Enquiry Concerning Human Understanding
Euthyphro
Fear and Trembling
Genealogy of Morals
Grounding for the Metaphysics of Morals
Leviathan
Locke's Second Treatise on Civil Government
Meditations on First Philosophy
Meno
Nicomachean Ethics
On Liberty
Phaedo
Philosophy of History
The Prince
The Protestant Ethic and the Spirit of Capitalism
The Republic
Sickness Unto Death
The Social Contract
The Symposium
Utilitarianism
Utopia

PHYSICS

1D Motion
2D Motion
Angular Momentum
Applications of Harmonic Motion
Applying Newton's Three Laws
Collisions
Conservation of Energy
Conservation of Momentum
Dynamics
Gas
Geometric Optics
Gravitation
Heat
Kepler
Kinematics
Light
Linear Momentum
Magnetic Forces and Fields
Newton
Optics
Orbits
Oscillations
Rotational Dynamics
Rotational Kinetics
Rotational Motion
Sources of Magnetic Fields
Special Relativity
Thermodynamics
Uniform Circular Motion
Vector Addition
Vector Multiplication
Vectors
Work, Energy and Power

POETRY

Coleridge's Poetry
Dante's Inferno
Dickinson's Poetry
Donne's Poetry
Eliot's Poetry
The Faerie Queene
The Flowers of Evil
Frost's Early Poems
Hopkins's Poetry
Keats's Odes
Paradise Lost
The Rape of the Lock
Robert Browning's Poetry
Shelley's Poetry
Songs of Innocence and Experience
Tennyson's Poetry
Whitman's Poetry
Wordsworth's Poetry
Yeats's Poetry

PSYCHOLOGY

Abnormal Psychology
Anxiety Disorders
Attention
Behaviorism
Brain Anatomy
Cognition and Perception
Cognitive Psychology
Developmental Psychology
Dissociative and Somatoform Disorders
Humanistic Psychology
Language
Memory
Mood Disorders
The Neuron
Neuropsychology
Perception
Personality
Problem Solving
Psychodynamic Psychology
Schizophrenia
Social and Emotional Psychology
Suicide

SHAKESPEARE

All's Well That Ends Well
Antony and Cleopatra
As You Like It
The Comedy of Errors
Coriolanus
Cymbeline
Hamlet
Henry IV Part 1
Henry IV Part 2
Henry V
Henry VI Part 1
Henry VI Part 2
Henry VI Part 3
Henry VIII
Julius Caesar
King John
King Lear
Love's Labour's Lost
Macbeth
Measure for Measure
The Merchant of Venice
The Merry Wives of Windsor
A Midsummer Night's Dream
Much Ado About Nothing
Othello
Pericles
Richard II
Richard III
Romeo and Juliet
Shakespeare's Sonnets
The Taming of the Shrew
The Tempest
Timon of Athens
Titus Andronicus
Troilus and Cressida
Twelfth Night
The Two Gentlemen of Verona
The Winter's Tale